This High,
Wild Country

CONTINENTAL DIVIDE →

Lower Waterton Lake

Maskinonge Lake

Middle Waterton Lake

Red Rock Canyon

Upper Waterton Lake

Crandell Lake

Waterton Townsite

Goat Haunt

Boundary Mountains

Bertha Lake

Starvation Ridge

Cameron Lake

CANADA/US BORDER

Kintla Lake

Upper Kintla Lake

Belly River

Cosley Lake

Elizabeth Lake

Chief Mountain

Otatso Creek

Slide Lake

Ptarmigan Tunnel

Bowman Lake

Altyn Peak

Quartz Lake

Lake Sherburne

Many Glacier

Swiftcurrent Creek

Wynn Mountain

Polebridge

Salamander Glacier

Logging Lake

Grinnell Glacier

Granite Park

Garden Wall

North Fork Flathead River

Preston Park

Going-to-the-Sun Road

Saint Mary Lake

Logan Pass

McDonald Creek

Heavy Runner Mountain

Trail of the Cedars

Reynolds Mountain

Avalanche Lake

Sperry Glacier

Gunsight Lake

Snyder Lakes

Hudson Bay Creek

Snyder Creek

Cut Bank Creek

Sprague Creek

Triple Divide Peak

Gunsight Pass

Atlantic Creek

Lake McDonald

Lake Ellen Wilson

Apgar

West Glacier

Mount Jackson

Nyack Creek

Pacific Creek

Marias Pass

Middle Fork Flathead River

Walton →

Two Medicine Lake

This High, Wild Country

A CELEBRATION OF WATERTON-GLACIER INTERNATIONAL PEACE PARK

TEXT BY Paul Schullery
ART BY Marsha Karle

UNIVERSITY OF NEW MEXICO PRESS • Albuquerque

14 13 12 11 10   1 2 3 4 5

Library of Congress Cataloging-in-Publication Data

Schullery, Paul.
This high, wild country : a celebration of Waterton-Glacier International
Peace Park / text by Paul Schullery ; art by Marsha Karle.
     p. cm.
Includes bibliographical references and index.
ISBN 978-0-8263-4602-5 (paper : alk. paper)

1. Waterton-Glacier International Peace Park (Mont. and Alta.)—
   Description and travel.
2. Waterton Lakes National Park (Alta.)—Description and travel.
3. Glacier National Park (Mont.)—Description and travel.
4. Waterton-Glacier International Peace Park (Mont. and Alta.)—
   Pictorial works.
5. Waterton Lakes National Park (Alta.)—Pictorial works.
6. Glacier National Park (Mont.)—Pictorial works.
7. Natural history—Waterton-Glacier International Peace Park
   (Mont. and Alta.)
8. Natural history—Alberta—Waterton Lakes National Park.
9. Natural history—Montana—Glacier National Park.
 I. Karle, Marsha.
II. Title.

F1079.W3S36 2010
978.6'52—dc22

                              2009042963

Completion of this book has been facilitated by the scholar-in-residence
program at the Montana State University Library, Bozeman.

For our mothers,
Dorothy Karle Griffith and Judith Schullery,
and in memory of our fathers,
Albert Karle and Stephen Schullery

Contents

Introduction

OF BEGINNINGS

Amid the jumble of peaks on the east side of Glacier National Park stands one that, though neither the tallest nor the most photogenic, may be the most symbolic. At barely eight thousand feet, Triple Divide Peak is lower than many of its neighbors, but a quirk of geography distinguishes it from the rest, for it is a central dividing point for North America. Rain and snow-melt run down its western slopes into Pacific Creek, from there into Nyack Creek and on out of the park, eventually to the Pacific Ocean. Water draining the east side of Triple Divide becomes Atlantic Creek, which flows into Cut Bank Creek, which leaves the park on its way to the Gulf of Mexico. Water running to the north creates Hudson Bay Creek, whose ultimate destination is indicated by its name. The great naturalist and conservationist George

Bird Grinnell didn't have to know about Triple Divide Peak in order to justify calling this region "the Crown of the Continent," but this one peak clinches the case beyond all doubt. Many things begin here.

But a fine appreciation for the rooflike nature of the landscape existed long before Grinnell published his famous "Crown of the Continent" article in *Century Magazine* in 1901. The ancestors of the people now living on the Blackfeet Reservation, which borders Glacier National Park on the east, knew this country better than most of us could ever hope to, and they called these mountains "the Backbone."

In some ways, the two thousand or so square miles of Waterton-Glacier International Peace Park have changed a lot since those names were applied, but most of the changes have been administrative; they show on the maps, but they don't show on the land. The core of what eventually became Waterton Lakes National Park was first set aside as part of a forest reserve in 1895, then became a small park in 1911, after which its boundaries changed several times. Many of us hope that recent proposals to increase its boundaries by up to another one hundred thousand acres into the upper Flathead Valley will be realized soon.

The land that became Glacier National Park likewise changed hands, plans, and boundaries a number of times, being included in the Lewis and Clark Forest Reserve in 1897 and becoming essentially the size and shape it is now when declared a national park in 1910.

Then, in 1932, in a profound and enduring gesture of goodwill between Canada and the United States, the two parks were linked as Waterton-Glacier International Peace Park. That, too, was the beginning of many good things, including a growing awareness of the genuine global significance of these landscapes: both parks were honored as Biosphere Reserves by UNESCO, Glacier in 1976 and Waterton in 1979, and Waterton-Glacier International Peace Park was named a World Heritage Site in 1995.

For me, it began in 1974, when I first traveled through Waterton-Glacier International Peace Park as a young man traveling cheap in a world of fresh wonders. With no effort, I can still recall a remarkable number of moments from that first visit. Some were barely impressions, but they stuck and still form much of my mental image of the place.

From a distance, even on that first visit, I saw this land as a combination of landscape and skyscape, where dark peaks rose into towering storm clouds that seemed like ephemeral shifting ridges atop the more

▲ *George Bird Grinnell*

substantial stone ones. From the very edges of the parklands, I was and still am struck by the feeling of entering a different world. I find that is a common experience at many national parks—an unfortunate statement on how the parks have become islands of wildness in a sea of something else—but nowhere is the abrupt transition from one world to another more pronounced than here.

▲ *Dipper*

Once well into the parks, I moved in anticipation of the next bend in whatever creek, trail, or road I was traveling. Few landscapes I know, outside of the winding slickrock mazes of the American Southwest, are so quick to surprise with grand new scenes, and even fewer do it on the scale of these parks.

At the same time, I now see that first visit as an unrelieved series of small revelations in natural history. I first saw a dipper, a favorite bird of mine, "fly" underwater at Avalanche Lake. I got my first close look at a blue

Red Rock Canyon

grouse by a rock wall on the Going-to-the-Sun Road. My first view of Red Rock Canyon—all those vivid strata just underneath the richly green, heavily flowered landscape—gave me a whole new appreciation for the term "buried treasure." Less pleasantly, that first visit taught me about the fierce tenacity of a tick once it has gotten a good professional grip on you, and about the startling array of ineffective remedies that well-meaning bystanders will recommend to someone so afflicted.

Other recollections usually only come back to me when I return to their source. There's a little wetland not far from Apgar where on that first visit I saw a moose, and though I didn't see another one there until 2008, I have always approached it with the reflexive thought, "Here's a good place for moose." I still can't drive past St. Mary Campground without remembering a delicate little mayfly, freshly emerged from the nearby lake and swept over to my campsite by the evening breeze, that alighted on my hand as I prepared some grim and best-forgotten bachelor dinner. Every time I approach Coppermine Creek, no matter the season, I involuntarily look for a certain little slope of pale paintbrush that caught my eye that first time. So strongly do these memories resonate that today when I pass these spots, I sometimes fail to keep my exultations to myself. My spouse, Marsha, patiently, even cheerfully, endures them—perhaps because she knows as well as I do how exciting all these things can be.

Other memories from that first visit are just plain weird. One night at Sprague Creek Campground, I "camped" in my little Super

Cow and Calf Moose

Beetle, the passenger side of which I'd converted into a bunk. That night the car was just a trifle tilted, with my head lower than my feet and aimed toward the lake. In the middle of the night I awoke from a terrifying nightmare of my car coasting back, into the dark water—a memory firmly enshrined in my personal Hall of Great Moments of Panic.

I can't really say why all these memories stay so fresh, especially considering the many hundreds of others that have been piled on top of them during subsequent visits. At the time I was hopelessly hooked on the magic of another mountain landscape—Yellowstone—but I knew immediately that this place was also worth a lifetime of attention and passion.

In 1971, when I first applied for work as a seasonal park ranger, I had to fill out a form listing my preferred choices among the parks. Though I have never regretted for a minute that I was hired by Yellowstone, it amuses me to remember that I listed Glacier as my first choice and Yellowstone as my second. At the time I'd only been to Yellowstone twice and had never even seen Glacier. But somehow Glacier just sounded better, perhaps because I figured it would be less crowded. I can't imagine how the years would have gone if Glacier had hired me rather than Yellowstone, but I imagine that Glacier would have given me just as good a start. It is, after all, very good at starting things.

Though I sometimes think that it was for the best that I made that first trip by myself—as if all those precious little discoveries were somehow better for making them solo—I never went back alone. That seems important to me whenever I reminisce about many later companionable experiences in the parks with friends and especially when I think of all the times that Marsha and I have shared in Waterton-Glacier in the past fifteen years. Already feeling spectacularly lucky to have discovered each other, we have been amazed at what a joy it is to discover—again and again, something new each time— Waterton-Glacier together.

▲ *Sacked-out Author*

Working Artist ▶

Marsha was already a national park veteran when we met in 1988. Her first two years as a "parkie" were spent in Denali, followed by assignments and details in Yellowstone, Denver, Hawaii, Mount Rushmore, Washington, D.C., and the Everglades. With that rich and varied exposure to wild landscapes and cultural treasures, she couldn't have been better prepared for Waterton-Glacier. With her passion for art and mine for writing, each of us seems always to be feeding the other's sense of the place, jumping at opportunities on each other's behalf. It's a great way to travel, and I see our two enterprises—my words and her art—telling two concurrent, overlapping, and complementary stories.

In that way, this book is much like the landscape it celebrates: lots of things happened to make it what it is, and the stories can be told in many ways. For each new visitor in each new generation, the first visit to Waterton-Glacier is another beginning in the adventure we share in this high, wild country.

◄ *Geraniums*

CHAPTER ONE

THRUSTS, FAULTS, AND OTHER GEOLOGICAL ACROBATICS

STONES

I have a habit in Waterton-Glacier that I have nowhere else. I pick up little rocks, study them for a minute, then look up to the mountains to find the parent of whatever little piece I hold in my hand. This leads me to consider all manner of connections and processes.

If I happen to be high on a dry slope at the time, the rock will be sharp and jagged—a freshly fallen, randomly faceted, coarse-surfaced little thing whose shape my mental processes of organization involuntarily attempt to recognize—an arrowhead, a cashew, a guitar pick, a badge. If it's flat (and most are flatter along one plane or another) I reflexively fit it into the curve between my thumb and forefinger, testing its heft and promise as a skipping stone, though I may be miles from open water.

If I happen to be loafing on the shore of a lake—let's say one of the long, deep ones that radiate out from the central mountain spines of the park—I find a whole different class of rocks. They have the same general assortment of shapes, usually flattened rather than round, and they come in the same colors, made much brighter by being wet. But their contours are softer. There are no sharp angles and edges, no fresh fractures, no raspy friction against the thumb. Again I look up to the mountains, to see if I can figure out where each piece started.

▲ *Rocks on Their Way Down*

I'm rarely sure I can tell. The sheer mountain faces two thousand or three thousand feet above me are splotchy, weathered, lichen-coated, and often deceptively lighted; none of them bear a lot of resemblance to the smooth, wetly shining little rock I hold in my hand. But I keep trying, and I suspect I make the right guess fairly often. That dark horizontal band there, about two-thirds of the way up, that the geology guidebooks would call green but looks to me like a kind of muddy slate; that's probably where this little rock came from.

Geology is a pretty hard sell for most people, because it demands so many leaps of faith. The geologist tells a story of biblical proportions, an epic tale of continent-sized plates of earth crust, moving with a speed that makes glaciers seem like cheetahs, ponderously slamming around the planet's surface, grinding into each other and setting off all kinds of titanic "lesser actions" on their surface—mountain building, volcanism, seas ebbing and flowing, and all the other side effects that we blink-of-an-eye mortals regard as a pretty big deal. It's hard to think of the Rocky Mountains, or even some individual mountain, as being merely minor consequences of bigger events, so by the time the geologist gets down to explaining what happened in a specific place, such as these two parks, we're so overwhelmed by the cosmic magnitude of the big picture that we can barely comprehend the local neighborhood.

But we're interested and almost pathetically eager to understand. So we follow the geologists and their guidebooks as they point at various spots on the landscape and give us a biography of the past billion or so years, confident that the visible proof of their explanation will be obvious to anyone with the sense God gave a goose. We listen intently. We nod our heads trustingly. But we reserve some doubt, and feel a little foolish asking them questions like, "Yes, but where did this little rock come from?"

No matter how often I read or hear the geological story, those small questions linger in my mind. Why is this rock green in the first place? How long does it take a rock to get from the top to the bottom? Do the rocks usually start out as big ones and break up on the way down? Do the ones breaking off today stand a chance of reaching the lake, now that there are so many other rocks piled up in the way? How much of the smoothing is done while the rock is on its way down, and how much is done after it comes to rest in the lake and is sloshed around with other rocks by a few thousand years of waves? And what happens next? Will all these rocks go somewhere else later?

▼ *Hoary Marmot*

THE LONG STORY

I don't blame the geologists for my bewilderment about geology, any more than I blame General Motors that I don't really understand automatic transmissions. And historically, my geological bewilderment put me in very good company here in Glacier. For more than a century now, distinguished explorers and geologists have been poking around here, gradually answering the really important questions, then reconsidering them, then answering them again.

As it happens, most of Glacier's geological history was fairly sedate. Practically all of the rock you see, whether attached to a mountain or easing its way down toward a valley bottom, was laid down as sediment at the bottom of various inland seas, layer upon layer, thousands of feet thick. This process started about a billion and a half years ago.

I never use numbers like these without mentally making sweeping gestures to indicate the staggering imprecision of what I'm saying— a billion here, a billion there, as the late Senator Everett Dirksen once famously put it while discussing the federal budget. Glacier's oldest rocks are from 1.6 billion to 0.8 billion years old and were all laid down in the Proterozoic Eon. After the Proterozoic, sediments continued to build up for another 300 million years or so, through the Paleozoic Era, but in Glacier none of the Paleozoic sediments survive today. They all have been eroded away during the past 200 million years, leaving only the much older rocks.

Another thing that makes us a little uneasy about the geological story is the ease with which the experts identify these ancient layers, mainly by the specific colors they see in them. They confidently describe rocks or whole strata as red, or yellow, or green, or any other obvious color, though the real hues are more subtle. Even the rocks that are only one predominant shade are rarely a simple, uniform color. The ones that are called red may actually be a nice, honest red, but most are more like a faded-brick red, or maybe a vegetable-soup red, or a mahogany brown, or some other equivocal shade. The yellows are often more like dusty tans, or old-chewing-gum-under-a-theatre-seat gray, than a real yellow. And the greens range from mint licorice to grasshopper green. Subtleties abound. But if you line the bottom of a shallow stream with a mixture of these rocks on a sunny day, you have a show superior to anything in Tiffany's window. Add the ethereal tinting of a milky glacial stream flowing over them, and they seem to exist in some extravagantly vivid dimension we're rarely privileged to glimpse.

A little chemistry helps us understand how all this came to be. The primary influences in making the original colors of the rocks are the amount of iron minerals involved in their creation and the depth of the water in which they were deposited. If they contained sufficient iron (usually in the form of hematite, but sometimes pyrite), and the water was shallow enough for oxygen to be available, the resulting color would be some variation on the rust theme: reddish, brownish, maroonish, even purplish. Greens and grays usually resulted from an oxygen-deprived environment (that is, formation occurred in deeper water, say, a hundred feet or more), where heat and pressure altered the chemical character of the rock, turning it into chlorite.

This summary is too tidy, though. As the ocean floor rose and fell, alternating bands of reddish and greenish rocks were created in the bed. With enough heat and pressure, both types became darker minerals—magnetite or biotite. The rocks least influenced by these various chemical processes are likely to be simple tans. To add to the difficulty of figuring out what the colors mean, all the rocks have been subjected to weathering, fading, and a variety of other influences, including lichens and mosses that obscure their colors.

Besides, the creation of these layers of rock results from more than just the simple deposition of sediment. Occasional subterranean

▼ *Glacial Stream Bottom*

▲ Salamander Sill

movements of molten earth, under fabulous temperatures and pressures, forced "sills"—layers of other material—between existing layers in the stack. Not only do these sills add yet another color (usually a very dark one) to the mix, but their intense heat also bleached out the sedimentary rocks above and below them, creating a pale "halo" along both sides of the sill. Among the most photographed sill locations is where it emerges from under the southern end of Salamander Glacier, above Grinnell Glacier in the upper Swiftcurrent Creek drainage.

Most of the rock in Glacier was put there before life got very complicated; these huge cliffs contain no dinosaurs or even fish ancestors to speak of. They do, however, contain countless fossils of algae, known as stromatolites, which lived in the shallower portions of the seas and are now visible at various places in the park (there are some visible right from the road as you begin to climb the west side of the Going-to-the-Sun Road, but it's a terrible place to stop the car and look). To the casual observer, they are evident as circular patterns and disruptions in the otherwise relatively straight strata. Some of the most pronounced are likened to cabbages and may be several feet across, revealed as twisting bulges and columns of rock. Where prehistoric conditions (presumably such things as nutrient availability, water temperature, and sunlight) were right for their colonies to grow, stromatolites thrived, and their fossils now exist in beds as much as one hundred feet thick.

Stromatolites bring geology down to a manageable personal scale for me. I picture myself poling a skiff through the shallows of some ancient bay, along the edge of one of these monumental plant communities as it dipped and rose in the gentle swells. But I wonder if there'd be enough oxygen for me that long ago, even with all the work these plants were doing cranking it into the atmosphere.

Here is a brief tour of the layers of sediment in Waterton-Glacier, starting with the oldest, which are on the bottom. The oldest visible formation in the two parks is the Waterton, which appears only on the Canadian side of the border. If you're hoping to identify this or any other formation by its color, the Waterton Formation shows how difficult this is. One geologist, in describing the Waterton, said, "Although a fresh surface is red-brown or gray, the dolomite weathers to gray, tan, or reddish brown." That's quite a range of colors, and it's only one formation.

The oldest visible rock—a billion or so years in age—on the American side, the Altyn Formation, is as much as 2,300 feet thick and is usually tan. It can only be seen on the east side of the park. Apparently (and I love this kind of historical imprecision), Altyn was the name of either an early miner or another early miner's horse. It may have been the name of both, but it's unclear for which the formation is named. The first 3,000 feet above the Altyn Formation is occupied by the Appekunny Formation, apparently named for James Willard Schultz, who lived much of his long life in the region and celebrated its wild country and native inhabitants in many very enjoyable books. The Blackfeet gave him this name (the preferred spelling for most purposes is Apikuni), which means "spotted robe." The formation is dominated by greenish and grayish shale-like rocks, known as argillites and siltites. Above it is the thinner (about 800 feet) and mostly gray Empire Formation. The

▼ *Stromatolites*

Grinnell Formation, named for the great naturalist and conservationist George Bird Grinnell (Schultz's friend), is layered above that, as thick as 1,400 feet, and is most known for some of the brightest, most obvious reds in the park. Grinnell, a great if inadequately celebrated naturalist and conservationist, is often credited with being the father of Glacier National Park, and this seems like the sort of monument he would have appreciated.

Above the Grinnell is the Helena Formation, 2,500 feet of grays and tans; the Prichard Formation, 4,000 feet of dark grays and near-blacks; the Shepard Formation, 600 feet of grays, greens, and yellows; and the Snowslip Formation, 1,400 feet of numerous pale shades that cap some of the most prominent peaks in the center of the park. Of all the formations, the Helena is the one with the most pronounced sills—haloed, dark gray bands toward the top of some of the most spectacular peaks.

If you were adding while you read the previous three paragraphs, you noticed that these layers total 15,000 feet of sediment. You may also know that the highest point in Waterton-Glacier is 10,466-foot Mount Cleveland, which rises only about 7,300 feet above Lake McDonald. So, you may wonder, how can there be 15,000 feet of sediments in 7,300 feet of elevation change? Good question.

THRUSTS AND FAULTS

About 65 million years ago ("give or take 10 million," as geologist Gary Alt has written), this landscape began to take on features recognizable in the modern park topography. The big event was the Lewis Overthrust, in which an enormous slab of these sediments, all the way down to the Altyn Formation, separated from its neighbors and from its foundation and began to move east. These masses are almost as incomprehensible as the time spans involved, but it went roughly like this.

Picture two boards, several feet long and a foot wide, aiming north and south. One lies directly on top of the other, and they are held together by a nail at the south end. The top board is the overthrust slab, whose northern end will move the greatest distance. Now push the top board toward the east; it will "hinge" at the nail. In the case of the Lewis Overthrust, the hinge is more than sixty miles south of the park, near the West Fork of the Sun River. Now picture the top slab moving away from the adjoining land to its west; a gap is created, quite a big one, that we now call the valley of the North Fork of the Flathead River, which runs along the west side of the park. When you drive up the west side to Polebridge, and stand munching some fabulous goodie baked at the store there, you're deep in that long trough. West of this ten-mile-wide valley, the Whitefish Mountain Range is composed of the same rocks, in the same layers, as those to the east, in the park. East of this valley, the slab moved on.

Now picture the low country east of the park—the Great Plains. From out there, as you drive west toward the park from Browning, Montana, you see ahead of you the Rocky Mountain Front, a wall of towering peaks and ridges with the magnificent "outlier" Chief Mountain at

▲ *Polebridge Mercantile*

the apparent north end of the row. The perhaps overly lyrical writers who describe mountains as seeming to march forward in ranks would not be far wrong here; you are looking at what's left of the leading edge—the "front"—of the overthrust slab, which marched this far and came to rest on younger rock. Marsha and I long ago agreed that this is by far our favorite way to approach the park, moving slowly across the rolling prairie onto the reservation and into Browning (with an obligatory stop for snacks and gas), then by any of the available routes toward that row of fantasy ridges and peaks that loom enticingly along the entire western horizon.

Geologists have now mapped the "fault," or the front edge, of this overthrust for more than 250 miles, from far south of the hinge to well into Canada. In some places, the total eastward movement of the slab was probably as much as fifty miles. The thickness of the material in the slab ranges from a few hundred feet down near the hinge to more than 6,000 feet up in the park.

The overthrust presented early scientific explorers with a pretty puzzle. When Bailey Willis and his colleagues came here in 1901, their most startling discovery must have been made along this front, where they found relatively young Cretaceous rocks, not much more than 100 million years old, resting directly underneath the billion-year-old Altyn Formation, which itself sat at the bottom of the pile of other formations, all much older than the Cretaceous. In 1902, Bailey formally recognized the nature of what had happened and named this mass the Lewis Overthrust.

But for all the motion of the overthrust, when it was more or less complete the land still bore only faint resemblance to its modern appearance. For the next 60 million years or so, it continued to change slowly. Streams carved steep canyons and tight little valleys into the sedimentary rocks, washing eroded material away to lower lands east and west. This process set the stage for the ice sculpting that gave us the present park area, but before getting to that, I should return to the earlier question; how can 15,000 feet of sediment be identified in a 7,300-foot-high mountain range?

Some parts of the answer are subtle: the formations are not always at their maximum thickness, and some of the higher ones are completely or largely gone, eroded away.

But the most important part of the answer is that the formations are not flat. They lie in a syncline, a huge concavity running north and south up the middle of the park. Seen in an east-to-west cross section, the formations visible in Waterton-Glacier are not a straight layer cake; they sag—a lot—in the middle, as if the cake had been supported only on its east and west edges and the middle had drooped like an old mattress. Thus, where they are exposed on the surface, the formations tend to slant inward, allowing a two-thousand-foot-thick layer, let's say, to gain only a few hundred feet in actual elevation.

ICE

Waterton-Glacier's scenery has exhausted the adjectival resources of many a writer. Some writers retreated into breathlessness, others strained toward some unachievable metaphorical power, and others collapsed into statistical security, incanting elevations and distances as if numbers could bring it all to life. But some writers, both technical and popular, have come pretty close to capturing the feel if not the scale of the place, usually when they compared what they saw with something more familiar. The sheared-off faces of the mountains can in fact remind you of the prows of ships, though ships the size of asteroids. The cirques, those lovely, high, little

Below Ptarmigan Tunnel

▲ *Mountain Pyramid*

mountain-backed coves, have repeatedly been compared with the work of someone with a giant ice-cream scoop, and a few are in fact perfect enough to have been left by such a device.

On the other hand, I have yet to see a mountain, here or anywhere else, that looked even faintly like a throne—whether royal or bathroom. Throne imagery—long a staple of descriptive writing in the canyon country of the American Southwest—has also been popular here, but I suspect that it only works because it evokes royalty, and there is something imperially grand about this landscape.

It took me years to sort out the faint sense of recognition these mountains gave me. I was occasionally aware that they were reminding me of something, but I just couldn't call it to mind. Then one day as I was looking at some slides taken on a backcountry trip, I suddenly had it. My hiking companion had photographed me standing soggily in the rain with a high and distinctly pyramidal peak behind me, and I finally just couldn't miss the comparison.

Though these mountains still don't remind me of the pyramids of Egypt, I was suddenly struck by their similarity to certain Mayan pyramids I'd seen nearly forty years ago at Tikal in Guatemala. With their stepped and often very steep sides, their intricate facades, and their flat caps, the Mayan temple-topped pyramids seem to me perfect stylized imitations of glaciated peaks. A few centuries of weathering, crumbling, and general collapse of the human-made pyramids of Central America have only made the similarities more pronounced. It causes me to wonder what the Mayan master builders would have made of this place if, at the height of their own construction activities, a few had found their way here. In a certain mood, it's nice to imagine that they did.

Two or three million years ago, the earth cooled enough for enormous sheets of ice to form over much of the northern and southern ends of the globe. There were a series of these events, or ice ages, the last one ending about eleven thousand years ago.

▲ *Upper Grinnell Lake*

A glacier is snow, fallen to great depths, packed to great mass, and brought to life by its own weight. More weight, more time, and more freezing-thawing cycles turn it to ice, which piles up until finally, at a depth of 150 to 200 feet, the whole thing begins to flow.

"Flow" is an important word here; the glacier doesn't just get heavy and slide down the hill. It takes on a kind of elasticity or flexibility, like liquid. Much like the water in a river, a glacier flows faster in the thick middle than it does on the thin edges and faster on the top side than on the bottom, which must contend with the snagging friction of the valley floor. It also flows faster at the head (the upper end), where the most new snow and weight are being added, and at the snout (the front, or lower end), where it is most subject to melting in the warmer lower temperatures, than it does in the middle. With all this animation and almost temperamental variability, it's easy to understand why we sometimes characterize glaciers as is if we were describing living things.

The glacier does its carving in all directions. At its head, the freezing and thawing along its boundary with the rock of the mountain allows the glacier to attach itself to solid rock, then, as it moves off a bit, pull that rock loose. Snowmelt refills the gap between the glacier and the mountain and turns to ice that attaches itself to the rock, and the process starts again. Ultimately, the glacier excavates and occupies a cirque, the large, rounded headlands that are so common on the upper faces of the mountains of the two parks.

Underneath, where the ice is moving over the land, the sole of the glacier (aptly comparable to the sole of a snail) similarly plucks rocks free. Once embedded in the sole, rocks grind away at the valley floor, abrading, scraping, and pushing along whatever is worked loose and leaving a network of scrapes, grooves, and other marks scattered on the faces of the mountains all over the park. On the sides and in front of the snout, the glacier piles up moraines—raw-looking ridges of loose rock that remind many people of construction sites, so uniform and gravel-like are the angular piles that remain when the glacier backs off.

During the last great Pleistocene ice age, glaciers in the park area worked their way down into the valleys, joining others to form mighty ice streams that eventually flowed out onto the open plains as wide-lobed piedmont glaciers. Working from the existing network of drainages, they defined and reworked the major valleys of the present park. Ten miles long and a thousand feet thick, they flowed west out of the park area, where they joined others coming south from British Columbia and east from the Whitefish Range, to fill the North Fork Valley with a giant glacier half a mile thick. Farther south, more glaciers flowed from the west side of the Lewis Range, joining in the valley of the Middle Fork along the present park boundary. Parts of this ice flow actually backed up over Marias Pass, thus crossing the Continental Divide and joining the Two Medicine Glacier, which emerged onto the plains along the southeast edge of the present park. Up along the east side of the front, glaciers spread out onto the prairie from the smaller valleys, while the valleys along the northeastern side of the park filled with north-flowing glaciers that moved up into Canada from the St. Mary Valley, the Belly River Valley, and others.

The most recent retreat of these glaciers was dramatic and, by geological standards, almost sensationally abrupt. Twenty thousand years ago, the spread of ice was at its greatest. Nine thousand years later, 90 percent of that incredible ocean of ice was gone, and only a relatively few high-elevation glaciers remained.

But we now know that even in the historical past the glaciers have come and gone. Most recently, following an extended warmer period of about four centuries during what we think of as the medieval period in Europe, the global climate cooled into the Little Ice Age, a five-century (give or take; authorities differ on its duration) interval that concluded about 1850, when the glaciers of the present park had again extended impressively.

There is an engaging irony in the Little Ice Age suddenly ending just about the time that European observers showed up. All over the nineteenth-century West, as white explorers, settlers, and researchers traveled, mapped, and studied the landscape, they were almost completely unaware that the plant and animal communities they encountered—and that they presumed were somehow "normal" for the region—were in fact artifacts of a climatic regime that had, by a remarkable coincidence, just ended. The changes in these natural settings that ensued following the end of the Little Ice Age continue to baffle people even today, especially when we try to use the conditions those first white explorers observed as some kind of measure of the purity or "pristineness" of these wild landscapes. Even if European humans hadn't overrun these landscapes and introduced huge and even catastrophic changes to the native plant and animal communities, the landscapes would have continued to change along their own climate-driven trajectories.

This sort of unanticipated variability in a park's natural setting adds considerable spice to the lives of managers, advocates, scientists, and anyone else engaged in trying to figure out how the place's wild setting should look and act now. Some people even try to use this ongoing natural variation in climate as an excuse to ignore the human-caused climate changes that have been so famously proven in recent years. People in denial about human-caused changes in the planet's climate now argue, unpersuasively I think, that the climate is just changing naturally. But understanding the distinction between these long-term natural changes and the sometimes spectacular changes brought on by industrial humans matters hugely, and national parks continue to offer us important lessons in how to measure those changes, in how to think about nature and our place in it.

Those enduring philosophical complications aside, we must consider the continued and ever more complicated saga of the glaciers—their comings and goings and their mighty contribution to the shaping of the landscape. During the Little Ice Age, at least 150 glaciers in present

Glacier National Park either grew in size or were created, filling many cirques and upper drainages. Together with the previous Pleistocene glaciations, these glaciers left a magnificent legacy.

What the glaciers left was an improbably steep land, where all motion seems up and down, a constantly side-hilling, ridge-running kind of place. With my hiker's urge to get to a different place from where I am, I see Waterton-Glacier as a realm of passes—slightly less high places that allow me to move from one wonderland to the next.

What the glaciers left was two large mountain ranges. The Livingston Range runs down the western half of the park from the Canadian border to Lake McDonald, while the Lewis Range runs the length of the park on the eastern side, from Canada to the gap we call Marias Pass. The streams flowing from these high ranges pool up in the narrow adjoining lowlands, creating on both sides of the park a series of long, roughly parallel lakes that give daily demonstrations of the pathetic inadequacy of the word "blue."

What the glaciers left was an intricate network of valleys, the comfortably rounded drainages characteristic of ice carving. The valleys usually head in one or more cirques, and sometimes one mountain will have three or even four cirques, turning its remaining peak, or "horn" (recall the Matterhorn), into a narrow, squared-off spire or pyramid. When two glaciers chew away the rock between them, leaving only a thin wall, it is called an arête; the best-known one in the parks is the Garden Wall, most easily visible from the Going-to-the-Sun Road on the west side and happily accessible by the highline trail, a magnificent if longish day hike from Logan Pass to the Loop just above McDonald Creek. Where an arête has been broken through and worn into a gentle saddle, it is called a col. Many if not most of the passes around the parks are cols.

▲ *Harlequins on Turquoise*

Where a small, high glacier once flowed into a much larger and lower glacier, the retreating ice often left a high valley that ends abruptly in a cliff. Such a place is called a hanging valley, and the parks are full of these, too—intimate and beckoning little paradises that often hide two or three small lakes and all sorts of other wonders and drain in one or two long waterfalls that plunge to the larger valley below.

What the glaciers left was one of the most tortuous, abrupt, and neck-straining drainage systems in North America. All those horns and cols and hanging valleys, with all their remaining snowfields and ice, shed the glacial melt and snowmelt and summer rain in long, waving threads of water that always surprise you as you approach them, their roar awakening you to their true size and volume. High-gradient streams, maybe beyond counting and certainly beyond naming, rush across the angled slabs of red and green and gray. They finally come to rest in lakes and ponds, from the smallest secret tarns resting in the remotest cirques to the long, landmark lakes that support a vast post-card industry.

RETREATS

What the glaciers left, however, was very little in the way of actual glacier. Those that remain continue to shrink and vanish, as do their counterparts elsewhere in the world. The warming trend that followed the end of the Little Ice Age in the mid-nineteenth century was forceful enough that many of the glaciers in what would become the park immediately began to retreat. By the early 1900s, this retreat was well known. Though the pace of the retreat has varied depending upon annual and decade-long variations in the warming trend, the glaciers continued to shrink until a brief hiatus caused by a slight global cooling trend, between 1950 and 1975, when glacial retreat around the world ceased and many glaciers even began to grow again.

But as today's headlines and a wealth of persuasive new research from around the globe remind us, glacial retreat has resumed, heightened by the growing intensity of human effects on the planet's atmosphere. Fierce resistance to this new and difficult reality among many policy makers and the public about global change seems to be worn down in stages. Just as for some years many people refused to acknowledge that the climate was changing but now accept that reality, so, too, they seem to need to pass through a stage in which they deny that the change might be our fault.

On the other hand, those of us who have been watching the steady refinement of scientific interpretation of these spectacular events for the past twenty or thirty years struggle with impatience at continuing resistance to the obvious. Waterton-Glacier and other places that protect relatively undisturbed natural settings have always had a lot to teach us, but never before has it been so urgent that we listen carefully.

The 1990s and the first decade of the new century have been the hottest on record, and the glaciers of Glacier National Park have responded with a furious pace of retreat. The 150 glaciers of 1850 became about 37 by 1966 and 26 today. Those numbers are impressive but hardly tell the whole story; something on the order of 90 percent of the volume of ice is gone. Those 26 remaining glaciers are typically much smaller (and thinner) than the glaciers of the nineteenth century.

And the change is picking up speed. The melting being documented today is substantially outrunning predictions of ice loss made in the 1990s.

The science and art of predicting how glaciers disassemble themselves have benefited tremendously from our century-and-a-half-long front row seat at the glacial retreat in Waterton-Glacier, but there are so many variables to be considered that precision is neither possible nor desirable in predicting how this will play out. Again, predictions must be modified. Computer modeling from the 1990s and as recent as 2003 suggested that if current climate trends continued, the last twenty-six increasingly slight glaciers in Glacier National Park would be gone by 2030. By early 2009, Dan Fagre, the U.S. Geological Survey researcher who has led so much exciting recent research on the changing glaciers of Glacier National Park, had revised that prediction to 2020.

If, on the other hand, the warming trend eases somewhat rather than continues, maybe some of the Waterton-Glacier glaciers may last until 2100. Whichever scenario prevails, if you want to see glaciers in action in the Northern Rockies, very soon you'll have to drive a good bit farther north—well into Canada, in fact—and the longer you wait, the farther north you'll have to drive.

The most striking part of our national conversation about the fate of the glaciers is how many people still don't seem to make the connection between this startling event and their own lives. National parks have always been perceived and promoted as great places of refuge from the hectic and often mean pace of everyday life, but they are not refuges from some imagined "real life." The glaciers of these parks mutely remind us of prospects and culpabilities that rarely confront us this baldly back home in town.

▲ *Cameron Falls*

Today's more alert observers liken the glaciers to familiar and even folkloric "listening posts" by which people have attended to their world. They are like the canaries once carried by miners; the canary's quick little respiration system registered finer changes in air quality than the miner might notice, and if the bird stopped singing or keeled over it was time to take notice. Today, those of us who respond to Waterton-Glacier's warnings with offhand comments—"Who cares about glaciers?"—are like the miners who ignored the canary and kept digging.

Gloomy as these deliberations sometimes get, they make it pretty obvious that the most important legacy the glaciers left is a landscape almost perfectly tailored to tell us about ourselves and the way we treat the planet. Our changing global environment is mirrored, and forecast, in many parts of these parks' landscapes, and I will return to them later.

Meanwhile, I return in memory to those little stones and the immense mother rocks they fell from. Standing on a high col—ducking behind a low screen of trees when a sleet storm passes through from the cirque I left to the cirque I now face—I alternately wonder about very little questions and very big ones.

I wonder if humans can last long enough for our effects on the climate to eventually show up in the same kind of phenomenally long stone biography I see reaching up the mountainside before me. Then I absently toe the rock rubble at my feet and wonder if all these little sharp-edged rocks, so fresh from their respective formations, will have to wait for the next glacier to come by before they can get down to the bottom.

And I'm not sure which is the big question and which is the little one.

Emerald Mountains

TENACITY AND SURRENDER IN THE FOREST

FROM THE PASS

The mixture of sleet and snow blows over, but I'm too cold standing still, so I abandon my rumination on the fate of the small stones at my feet and get moving. I'm only good for a little while with the big questions—then I need to concentrate on simpler things, like trying to figure out a way to extract junk food from my pack without bothering to take it off my back.

On this trip, I'm actually following an expert, National Park Service biologist Steve Gniadek. (Since this trip, we have both retired from the agency, but in the 1970s Steve and I worked together in Yellowstone, then went separate

Pileated Woodpecker

ways, his eventually taking him to Glacier and a long productive stint when he exercised his passions for wilderness, especially its bird life.) I will complete this hike with a random pile of impressions and many poorly framed photographs; he'll take back a careful inventory of avian information. We take a last look down into the cirque we've just climbed from and prepare to head down the trail.

But it's impossible to stop looking out, way out—far away from where I stand. This landscape is always grabbing you and spinning you around, demanding that you absorb yet another fantasy vista and consider yet another beckoning pass astride some distant ridge.

From where I have been sitting, at about 7,000 feet, peaks rise abruptly on both sides of the pass, all raw rock, lingering ice, and a little fresh snow and sleet from earlier today. Scanning the high mountains and walls to the east, where we are heading next, I think I can discern a cirque-like character to things, but I could be looking into parts of two or three different ones. I'm sure that the country we must descend through is the result of glaciers, but there are no textbook-neat, rounded-out alcoves presenting themselves from this viewpoint. It's all more ragged than that, with distant ribbons of ice melt undulating off vertical faces. The whole convoluted bowl before me drops off out of sight at an angle to the northeast, where I can't see its course or its contours. At my feet, grayish snowbanks, dwindling with almost visible reluctance in the equivocal late-spring weather, wind in long narrow curves along the ridge and up into sheltered pockets at the base of the cliffs. There's life up there, but not much.

ZONE WALKING

For many years, biologists and ecologists have divided dramatic landscapes like this into life zones, broad horizontal bands of organic communities draped over the inorganic layers of earth and stone. And if the geological layers seem jumbled and puzzling, the organic ones approach the chaotic, getting less easy to visually define and mentally pigeonhole the farther downhill you get. Biologists Vernon and Florence Bailey, in *The Wild Animals of Glacier National Park* (1918), a classic of the park's scientific literature, admitted right off that "only by a broad view can the zonal arrangement be recognized." As near as I have been able to tell, most of the time the "broad view" is the view one gets from several miles off—like from this pass.

Clements Mountain

The highest zone, starting just above me, is the most visually commanding and least hospitable. The walls, cliffs, horns, and other sheer rock forms draw our eyes away from the low country. From any distance, the cliffs look bare, with no potential for plant life. But a variety of mosses and lichens do just fine up there. In the countless little niches and cavities and crevices that pock the sedimentary layers, other plants get by, too, maybe a sparse tuft of grass here, a stunted shrub or subalpine fir only a few inches high there.

We're walking more or less at the treeline here near the pass, the upper limit of marginal hospitality for such large and needy plants. In the park, treeline varies by more than a thousand feet, depending upon local conditions, including steepness and substance of the slope, wind, and aspect (which direction the slope faces, north being the harshest climate but also the wettest).

Up here, where the inorganic landscape is at its most baldly monumental, everything alive is in miniature. There are temporarily luxurious mats of "cushion growth," where a variety of ground-hugging herbaceous plants cover whatever soil they can find. Some of the most sensational, if subtle, flower shows occur here among the many "bellyflowers" (so named because you have to get on yours to enjoy them). I wasn't keeping good notes the day of this hike, but one of my photographs shows a big muddy hiking boot (possibly in the picture to provide a sense of scale, but maybe just by mistake) along the edge of a grand, vivid patch of moss campion, whose tiny blossoms were once known as mountain pinks.

A few hundred yards down the trail from the pass, we cross a sloping meadow thick with glacier lilies, whose little bulbs are a favored bear food (as if I needed yet another reminder to keep watch for bears). The trees at these elevations—usually some mixture of subalpine fir, whitebark pine, and Engelmann spruce—make a living by conceding every possible authority to their environment. Most of all, they are small and short and make many accommodations to survive.

Waterton-Glacier's timberline is a fantasy world of miniature forests. Stunted by extreme winds and frost (the latter working on the roots, as well as on the exposed limbs), desiccated by chinook winds and strong sun, with all their branches pennanted out on the side away from the wind, the trees take on a "krummholz," or shrublike form.

Some are "flagged krummholz," so named because they've gained enough height that the greenery on their top—the "flag"—pokes above the winter snows and is pounded by winter winds. The characteristic shape of this form is a low, full bush with a tuft-topped stalk a few feet high emerging from it.

Others are "cushion krummholz," packed low to the ground and often quite dense. Many trees develop "skirts" that reach out around the tree at ground level, or bunch together in narrow "tree islands" around some unusually sturdy individual, whose shade and shelter may foster a mini-forest of several species, huddled together for such shared benefits as wind and temperature screening and structural reinforcement against the wind.

Perhaps because they are so reminiscent of tiny fantasy forests in childhood tales, or perhaps because their small size makes them so easy to enjoy as somehow complete scenes, these little woods never fail to charm me. The first stream crossing, over a willow-bordered little stairstep of pools, has a Japanese garden perfection. It's a bonsai landscape of such extraordinary beauty that I instantly reach that peculiar desperation that comes from knowing something will completely resist being preserved in photographs. All I can do is look at it, surrender to its wonder, and go on.

All around us are signs of Bailey's broad view, which sometimes is surprisingly local. At this latitude, north-facing slopes are cooler than south-facing ones. The north slopes hold moisture longer. Thanks to the generally west winds of this region, snow tends to pile up more on the north slopes as well, giving them even more of a moisture advantage. These changes in the qualities of habitats on different aspects of each mountain add another dimension to the life zone picture. The warmer, drier south slopes tend to have higher timberlines.

The cynical chaotician in Michael Crichton's science-fiction thriller *Jurassic Park* said it all when he observed that "life finds a way." Life's capacity to spread and make itself at home is the defining characteristic of the biosphere. Given only oxygen, the slightest source of nourishment, and some little thing to hold onto, life appears in the most improbable places, from miles deep in the oceans to the highest peaks and beyond.

▲ *Cheeky Chickadee*

The life zone concept is convenient and, used carefully, true to the reality you find when you climb from the prairie to the high passes, but its appreciation requires a generous tolerance for imprecision. Cross the park west to east, and you will find striking changes in the placement of the zones, as moisture regime and prevailing winds change. Circle a single mountain from one side to the other, and you may find the zones shifting downward or upward hundreds of feet in response to exposure to sunlight or wind. Climb in and out of a deep ravine, and you may find remarkably different life communities on one side or the other, depending upon each side's exposure.

In fact, such looseness is part of the wonder of life here. Climb from the lowest elevation to the highest, and you will see that the zones do not have clear boundaries; in fact, life exists here in a continuum, not in tidy bands of different communities. As you move up, you will notice that plants that we consider characteristic of one zone straggle up and down the trail above and below that zone. Animals move all over the place, so that ground squirrels scurry around near the high passes as well as in the prairie grasses, and mountain goats may make their way from their famous high haunts to the river bottoms now and then, especially if they know of a good mineral lick down there.

But for all that diffuse interaction of life communities on the slopes of these mountains, the life zone concept is an important key to understanding life in the parks. Most of the time, most places, it's fairly easy to tell which zone you're in. There's no mistaking prairie meadow, or krummholz, or least of all the highest crags of raw rock. There's also no mistaking the preferred habitats of the larger animals. The mammals drift up and down this landscape rather like the snowline that some of them follow in their search for food; the grazers seek forage at its peak of nutrition, and the predators seek the grazers. But each species does so in a manner that is, if observed long and carefully enough, predictable and sensible. The arrangement of homes and food supplies and appetites is no accident here. It is the result of thousands of years of sorting out the possibilities, as all these separate but connected lives find their way.

▼ *Columbian Ground Squirrel*

This stormy day, Steve and I drop quickly down the switchbacks into heavier and heavier vegetation. At about 6,400 feet we pass a small unnamed pond. I look up and even with my nongeologist's eye, I can discern several distorted cirques from which ice once descended to round off all the contours around and below us. Some of them still contribute their meandering trickles to this pond, while others send their water off on adventures in other directions that I can't visually track from here.

A few more switchbacks down the face of small cliffs, and we're well below 6,000 feet and clearly into the next stage of Bailey's "zonal arrangement," the coniferous forests that cover about two-thirds of the park. Here on the east side of Glacier, the most common trees are lodgepole pine, Engelmann spruce, Douglas fir, and subalpine fir, with pockets (some large) of aspen, cottonwood, and other deciduous trees. On the west side, for reasons I'll get to presently, there are more and different kinds of trees—western hemlock, western red cedar, western larch, paper birch, and a batch of others, in addition to those most common on the east side.

In one open area, as Steve goes on ahead, I pause long enough to take yet another unsuccessful photograph of Indian paintbrush. Sometimes I think it's my favorite flower, if one can have a favorite among such a rich array of choices. Here, the paintbrush is given stiff competition by the yellow columbines, yellow violets, fleabane, and one of the billion or so daisylike flowers that, much like the sparrows in the bird world, all look different to me but not in any memorable way. As usual, however, the paintbrush gets most of my attention. Ever since that first visit to Glacier, I've been entertained by the seemingly endless number of shades of its paintbrush—rose, salmon, fuchsia, amber, candy apple red, arterial scarlet, baby-girl pink, canary yellow, lavender-gray—on and on through all the countless variations on red and pink and yellow. Paintbrush is my botanical equivalent of all those delicately shaded stones shining up at me from the shallow streambeds around here.

▲ *Paintbrush*

Catching up with Steve and continuing down the trail and down the slope, we're soon into brush and undergrowth that is both higher and denser than the stunted krummholz forest up above. Coming from a drier part of the Rockies farther south, I'm unaccustomed to so much lushness under the tree canopy and make lame jokes about the "cow-parsnip forest" as we walk past enormous versions of this plant that are

False Hellebore

taller than I am, mixed with devil's club, thimbleberry, alder, and false hellebore. Here and there, even in fairly heavy forest, beargrass towers over much of the undergrowth, its many tiny flowers forming a large, white, rounded cone as much as ten or twelve inches long. Many of these cones are not straight but bend to one side and then swoop up, giving an impression, when seen in a group, of a floral ballet caught in mid-dip.

As we drop to five thousand feet and skirt a couple of larger lakes, we wind up as close to the "bottom" as you can get on this side of Glacier, following a river through a series of long meadows. After two days of rain (each time a new wave of the storm hits us, one of us mutters, "'Tis but a squall . . ."), the sun finally emerges, and the now-receding peaks look more inviting than they did when we were among them. We cross a stream, then in a while stop to soak our hot feet in it, quietly watching the mountains we've just left as if we hope they'll show us one more thing we've missed so far. We're nearly to the car, but if we continued on

Beargrass Ballet

east beyond it, before long we would be out on the prairies of the Blackfeet Reservation. At several points along the east side of the park, a "transition zone" of upland prairie crosses into the park, adding its birches, aspens, willows, and various prairie grasses and wildflowers (the nearby signs welcoming us to Alberta remind us that it is wild rose country) to the park's cross section of life communities. At the prairie's edge, you cross that other, much less celebrated timberline—the lower limit of the forests.

The quickness with which one moves from one of these communities to another in the park is what has always distinguished Waterton-Glacier in the eyes of naturalists, and what helps make it so valuable to scientists today, to whom the park's vertical array of life zones provides a vivid and compact study area for tracking climate-induced changes in plant communities. These very different worlds are packed together for our convenience in only a few miles of trail.

▲ *Wild Roses*

The scale of it all changes abruptly at this point, though. We passed through them all in just a few miles, but once you're out on the prairie, it's about a thousand miles or so east to the next zone.

EAST SIDE, WEST SIDE

I suspect that many casual observers, driving across the middle of the park—say, from east to west—don't notice any change in the vegetation from one side to another. They almost certainly notice the change from dense forest to subalpine scrub as they climb up toward Logan Pass and back down, but their reaction to the drive is probably more on the scale (if not the sweeping eloquence) of the famous novelist Thomas Wolfe's commentary, made during a 1938 visit only five years after the Going-to-the-Sun Road was opened:

> . . . back again from St. Mary's crossing and the cabins along the Going to the Sun Pass and the stupendous hackled peaks now—the sheer basaltic walls of glaciation, the steep scoopings down below, the dense vortices of glacial valley slopes and forest—and climbing climbing to the Logan Pass so down again terrifically,

▲ *Going-to-the-Sun*

and the glacial wall beside, the enormous hackled granite peaks before, the green steep glaciation of the forest, the pouring cascades, and the streams below—and down and down the miraculous road into the forest, and by rushing waters, and down and down to the Lake McDonald and Hotel.

Setting aside Wolfe's geology problems (he wouldn't have seen basalt or granite, though he was fairly typical in thinking he did), he gives us a good idea of what impresses most one-day travelers. With all the hackled peaks and miraculous roads, who will notice subtlety?

In Waterton-Glacier, subtlety is spelled moisture. From the smallest bog to the grandest streamside cottonwoods to the tenacious lichens clinging to the highest crests, moisture is making many decisions about what life will do.

The one-sentence explanation of plant life here runs something like, "The west side is wetter than the east side, so it has different vegetation." This is a good start, but actually, and predictably, the situation is a great deal more involved. To begin with, this explanation gives the impression that the winds coming across the country from the coast hang up on the Continental Divide in Glacier, dump their precipitation on the west side, and have little left for the east side or the prairie beyond. Sounds like a classic rain shadow effect, and it happens, but it isn't all that's going on.

In fact, by most of the common climate indicators, there isn't much difference between the west and east sides. Take precipitation. Polebridge, up the valley of the North Fork on the west boundary, and Lake Sherburne, directly across the park on the east boundary, are within a third of an inch of each other in annual precipitation. Farther south, two other opposing villages, West Glacier and East Glacier, are within half an inch of each other in precipitation. Similar parallels prevail in average temperatures and relative humidity. The differences between the two sides must be sought in other factors.

One difference is the wind, especially winter wind. While you can count on exceptional, even extraordinary winds on the peaks anywhere in the park, the east side, from Waterton Park down through Glacier, gets some amazing winter winds through its narrow valleys. They are not always cold (this country being famous for its warm chinooks that briefly melt midwinter snows), but they are powerful. The published and unpublished lore of the parks is replete with tales of astonishing winds. St. Mary recorded gusts of 100 miles per hour in December 1979, as did Many Glacier a year later, but in 2006 a gust was measured at 164 miles per hour at Marias Pass near the south boundary of Glacier National Park.

High winds may damage plants simply by breaking or ripping off their limbs, but they have other effects, too. We think of drought as a hot, dry phenomenon, but it also occurs in the cold, when strong, arid winds dehydrate a tree's branches (a process heightened by strong sunlight). While these violent winds are pummeling every exposed living thing and desiccating soils and plants on the east side, over on the west side things are quiet, especially in winter, when the year's lightest winds pass through.

For a really easy and persuasive look at the effects of these winter winds, take a ride northwest from Babb, up the Chief Mountain International Highway toward the Canadian border. You'll drive for miles through beautiful but very short aspen forests. These forests stretch for miles across the lower ridges of the foothills of the Rocky Mountain Front. This is a hard place to be an aspen, but apparently

Larches

the soil is so accommodating that the species thrives in great abundance—grove after grove of gnarled, dwarfish trees with the tiny leaves that characterize aspen in its most extreme environment. In the fall, when these aspens turn blazing gold, their only rivals for autumn photogeneity in the park are the pale yellow larch forests that stretch up and down the North Fork Valley on the park's opposite boundary.

But wind isn't the only difference between the west side and the east side. Another is elevation. The valleys on the east side tend to be considerably higher than those on the west, and as my little life zone excursion at the beginning of this chapter suggests, it doesn't take much change in elevation to make a big change in vegetation. The biggest west-side lake, St. Mary, at 4,484 feet elevation, is significantly higher than its east-side counterpart, McDonald, at 3,153 feet.

And so, yes, the west is different from the east, and Lake McDonald is probably most different of all. Here, low elevation and a moist, moderate climate combine to create a coastal vignette, a Pacific Northwest forest of western hemlock and red cedar. When I walk the lakeshore, or hike up the Avalanche Lake trail, I am carried in memory to paths along favorite West Coast salmon rivers, in Oregon and Washington, and the shorelines of southeastern Alaska. Here along the hushed and damply soft trails of this forest, more than in any other forest in either park, I understand why people treasure and revere ancient forests.

▲ *Avalanche Creek*

DISTURBING SCENES

Wild ecosystems are incredibly flexible. The days are gone when nature was seen as a rigid biological machine proceeding soldierlike through various stages of growth, plant succession, and even evolution with a clearly determined course. In Waterton-Glacier, the evidence that nature doesn't work that way is everywhere. The scrambling of the geological layers and the constant tangling of the vegetation layers on top of them tell the story. It's a glorious mess.

Consider avalanches. When a batch of new rock breaks loose high on a cliff, or some growing imbalance finally puts an existing pile of loose rock beyond its angle of repose, an immediate corporate reorganization is undertaken. The 1968 Slide Lake rockfall avalanche, on the north side of Yellow Mountain (the large complicated ridge immediately south of Chief Mountain), measured more than a mile from the base of the mountain to where its leading edge came to rest in the channel of Otatso Creek (which it dammed, creating Slide Lake). Upward of a square mile of the mountain's lower slopes, all the way down to the riparian zone of the creek, was covered to a depth of several yards with new stone. That's habitat alteration at its most dramatic, and it happens frequently at more modest scales all over these mountains.

Snow avalanches make a lot more headlines, probably because they happen on a time scale we can better appreciate and thus are more likely to kill some of us. Their effects are also more easily recognized on heavily vegetated landscapes, especially in places where they recur often. Avalanche chutes are the contrarians of this landscape, going against the grain of both the geological and vegetation layers that at least roughly follow horizontal contours. You can't miss them; as you hike a trail along the side of a steep slope, you suddenly emerge into a shrubby, treeless meadow, one that runs clear from treeline down to the bottom of the grade.

The scientific literature of snow avalanche processes counsels great caution in interpreting what has happened in such a place. The vegetation you see is probably not merely what has sprung up since the last avalanche. These chutes tend to favor certain kinds of plants (such as really springy ones and those that might survive extended snow burial). These chutes also might host a great variety of snowslides—maybe a big one that sweeps the whole chute one year, then a little one that winds down a central gully the next, each one affecting the vegetation differently.

Avalanche Chute Bears

If you see an obvious avalanche chute, try this: after taking a good look up at what the avalanche did to the landscape as it came down the mountain, turn around and try to figure out what effect it had on the flat country. Sometimes the most impressive effects are out there, or even partway up a slope on the opposite side of the valley; the snow can go a long way uphill on the momentum from such a steep launching.

No less dramatic and a lot more controversial, fire is another great reorganizer of wild landscapes. During the famous Yellowstone fires of 1988, Americans may not have learned a lot about fire ecology, but they were suddenly a lot more aware that big fires are still a part of our world. Glacier had what by most standards would be regarded as a big fire in 1988, too. The Red Bench Fire caused more property damage than any other fire in Montana that year, but at "only" 23,000 acres it was not noticed by the national media, which were more interested in the hundreds of thousands of acres of burns in Yellowstone.

Glacier's equivalent of Yellowstone's 1988 fires came during the much more disruptive and visible fires of 2003, one of the hottest summers in the park's history, when the fire perimeters contained more than 140,000 acres. The six fires and fire complexes (groups of fires that joined in one or were fought under one name) caused a series of evacuations and temporary closures of this or that part of the park, stressing park staff, regional communities, and visitors alike.

A big fire is an enormous strain on the economic and emotional resources of a human community. The administrative overdrive that must be sustained during a major fire season is somewhere beyond exhausting for the professionals in charge of the lands involved. My sympathy for many of these sturdy souls is beyond expressing. But I must admit that when I got my first look at some of these burns the following year—even though the close calls suffered by park developments were all too evident—I was immediately absorbed in all the exciting things the fires had initiated on the wild landscape. I've been in Glacier a few times during fires, but my only contact with them was the sight of vivid red sunrises through drifting smoke, or a small flame seen off at a distance. The fires of 2003 demanded much more attention, and still do. Getting my first look at them the following summer, visually following the tracks of fire—the black with brown "halo" of recent burns—that must have been spectacular in action, I found myself imagining how that forest will look each year as more and more of the tall, dead snags fall and a new generation of trees slowly grows to replace them.

The ecological realities of these wildland fires have become almost clichés among modern naturalists interpreting wilderness values. Practically every life community in Waterton-Glacier, including the aquatic ones, evolved to its present form in the presence of fire. Fire shapes and recycles these communities. And all of those variables that influence the geological and vegetative settings come into play after the fire has passed, so that soil, slope, aspect, moisture, wind, and other inorganic processes affect the character of the new community.

In the mid-1990s, while Steve Gniadek and I were hiking to a wolf-rendezvous site on the west side of the park (where I happily settled for the sighting of some wolf scat, the wolves being somewhere else), we passed through a young stand of lodgepole pine. I was shocked to realize that they were six-year-olds that had come up since the Red Bench Fire; shocked, because some were as tall as I am, while down in Yellowstone, few six-year-olds had reached my waist yet. Even now, more than twenty years after the fires of 1988, there are still some sizable patches of these "new" forests in Yellowstone that are shorter than I am. But only a few years after the Red Bench Fire, the tops of the trees were well out of reach. Such are the vicissitudes of soil and moisture from one area to the next.

PRESTON PARK

Late one October, Kate Kendall, a longtime U.S. Geological Survey ecologist and friend, invited me to join her and a group of Nature Conservancy staff and members on a hike up to Preston Park, a cirque reachable by a short, steep walk from the Going-to-the-Sun Road a few miles east of Logan Pass. The snow was several inches to a foot deep, so the group "postholed" along, each putting his or her feet in the deep tracks of the person in front.

    We encountered all the usual wonders along the way: day-old black bear prints in the soft snow, unforgettable views of the "back" side of the Garden Wall, the looming presence of Matahpi Peak, and, when we stopped near the lake below Siyeh Pass, a long-distance view southwest to Reynolds Mountain. Our enjoyment of the country was all the keener because it was so obviously poised on the edge of winter—and so obviously soon to be out of reach by foot traffic like ours.

    Kate took us there to tell us about the park's whitebark pine trees. She pointed to the large stands of this tough, handsome tree, making sure we noticed how many dry gray snags protruded from the groves. In harsh environments like this, and in any forest where fire is allowed, one expects such snags, so a hiker coming on them unexpectedly might not have given them much thought. But, as Kate explained to us, white pine blister rust, a non-native disease, was gradually killing the whitebark pines. Glacier

▲ Forest Fire Stringers, Lake McDonald

National Park appears about to lose almost all of this species. To Kate's audience, made up of people from many disciplines but all at least vaguely aware of the ecological shocks that resulted from such events, this was a matter for great sadness and alarm. The loss of this species of tree, beyond its own aesthetic worth, will ripple through these high elevations with grave consequences. The power and reach of those ripples is certainly a reason that white pine blister rust is known among forest pathologists as "one of the most famous forest diseases in the world."

It is accurate, but dismayingly understated, to say that these are beautiful trees and that the high forests of Waterton-Glacier will be visually diminished by their disappearance. A wide accumulation of research over the past few decades makes it certain that the losses reach

▲ *Miss November*

far beyond changes in the photogeneity of any park scene. Whitebark pine is extraordinarily important in these higher-elevation life communities. Animals as large as grizzly bears and as small as jays and nutcrackers build significant portions of their annual food habits around it, and though none of these animal species will necessarily disappear from the parks entirely, some have already shown signs of the severe stress of losing such a crucial food source. In the subtle and interwoven relationships of plant communities of these harsh environments, the whitebark pine is one of the species whose establishment may create a windbreak in which other species can then take hold. The countless small environments maintained by all those shrubby krummholz, with their subtle influences on everything from soil nutrients to wildlife shelter, will be subjected to whatever adjustments the loss of the whitebark pines requires. All this brings to mind, and verifies, those vivid clichés about nature's web of life. White pine blister rust is both shredding and reweaving that web.

In his splendid recent book, *Glacier: A Natural History Guide* (2007), naturalist David Rockwell emphasized how far along this process has already progressed:

> It is rare now to see a cone on a whitebark pine tree in Glacier. In fact, it is estimated that nearly half of the whitebark pine trees in

the park are dead. Of the living trees, 78 percent are infected with rust, and more than a quarter of their cone-bearing crowns are now dead.

It is worth pointing out that though humanity's intentional and unintentional translocation of non-native organisms around the planet—a process that historian Alfred Crosby aptly labeled "ecological imperialism"—has been enormously complicated, the arrival of white pine blister rust in the Western Hemisphere, especially in Waterton-Glacier, is one of the more ironic chapters in this saga. In the late 1800s, when U.S. lumber manufacturers realized that their cutting of American forests could not go on indefinitely without replenishing the supply, German and French tree nurseries, which were far ahead of us in the culture of seedling production, began to produce eastern (American) white pine seedlings for sale back to American foresters. Blister rust was a fact of life among European foresters, so the seedlings were unavoidably infected. Thus it was that non-native blister rust made its way to America by riding in a native North American plant, then spreading from the East Coast (where it arrived in about 1898) and the West Coast (where it arrived in 1910) inland by means of infection.

▲ *Clark's Nutcracker*

A landscape's wildness is a matter of degree, and sometimes we can give that wildness a nudge back toward a more wild state. National Park Service staff in Glacier have been experimenting with restoration of whitebark pine even before it is gone. Collecting seeds from uninfected trees in infected stands, they are propagating these apparently resistant trees and thus keeping the species going in the park. It may seem like a small step, but given the long lives of whitebark pine, it also seems not a moment too soon to be trying such things.

Like it or not, humans are a big and very active part of even the wildest North America's landscapes. More than 10 percent—that is, more than a hundred—of Glacier's thousand or so species of flowering plants are not native; we've added them to this setting in the past century or so. Most have little measurable effect on the functioning of the native plant and animal community; others have dramatic effects; others may have effects we haven't even considered or noticed yet. Already, in difficult to articulate ways, we have lessened the magic of this place, and we have set in motion processes that continue to do so. For now, this knowledge makes Glacier seem all the more precious.

Crossed Trails

THE COMPLICATIONS OF WILD LIFE

MANY GLACIER

At dawn one day in late May, as I turned off Highway 89 at Babb and headed up toward Many Glacier, the distant snowy slopes in the park looked about the same as they had that day at Preston Park, but this was the opposite end of winter. Down south in Yellowstone, the early tourist season was already under way, but here there were no signs of the bustle and society that occupy this road all summer. It was cold, windy, and spitting snow—close to my ideal conditions for watching wildlife. It's not that you have to have

51

▲ *Many Glacier Hotel and Wynn Mountain*

bad weather to see animals, but if you do have it, you can count on them not having been spooked by others. Besides, as selfish as I must admit it is, there's something special in seeing wildlife alone.

Many Glacier is always a great place to look for wildlife, but it was especially generous this day, though every building in the place was still locked up from the winter. A mile east of the development, a mule deer doe stood on a rise above the road in front of me just before I noticed a cow elk farther back on the edge of a small aspen grove. As I passed the lane to the hotel, a white-tailed doe ran across the road in front of me.

At 6:35, I parked in the big empty parking lot in front of the Swiftcurrent Lodge, slipped the spotting scope mount over the car window, and began to scan the slopes rising in all directions. Right away, I saw a single mountain goat partway up Grinnell Point, the eminence to the south. Ten minutes later, four mule deer came out onto the parking lot and watched me for a while before turning back into the trees. A minute later, scanning the steep cliffs of Altyn Peak to the north, I saw a second goat, and then a cow elk appeared in the brush just above and behind the lodge. Scanning to the northwest, I found a herd of eleven bighorn sheep settled in a high ravine, well above the heavy cover; from their position, they had at least some shelter from the wind without having their view blocked in any direction. As I watched them, they started to move off in various directions, so I visually followed the ravine up and up to the cliffs above it, where I picked two more goats from the goat-sized patches of old snow.

At 6:52, I saw what I was most looking for. A grizzly bear sow became partially visible, moving through the scrubby vegetation only a little way up the slope behind the lodge. Over the next few minutes, her two cubs revealed themselves in disappointingly brief intervals, and then the whole family settled down in a little grove of mixed brush, aspen, and evergreens. Though I saw parts of them now and then over the next half hour, I never got such a good look again.

▲ *Bighorn Sheep*

I kept watching through the occasional snow shower, losing my view as curtains of snow and sleet swept across the higher slopes. Then, about 7:30, I drove half a mile or so back to another pullout that allowed me to scan the mountains southeast of Many Glacier.

Here, I really appreciated a strong scope, which can bring large mammals three or four miles away to a recognizable size. I soon picked out a big lumbering form in some high meadows on Wynn Mountain: another grizzly bear, this one probably a big male, judging from its

proportions and general massiveness. I watched him wander around for about fifteen minutes; he spent most of his time with his nose to the ground, grazing or digging or maybe just snuffling the possibilities. After many years of watching them, I am still surprised at the extended periods of inaction even a standing bear will endure for reasons I cannot discern.

Then, fairly well exhilarated with my good fortune at seeing so much activity, I headed back to St. Mary for some coffee and a hot shower. Marsha should be up by now and I couldn't wait to tell her about everything. That evening, we returned together, and to the morning's list of species we added a young bull moose with his antlers in velvet, about halfway between Babb and St. Mary.

Thinking back on that day, it occurs to me that these big mammals had displayed themselves with almost travel brochure perfection. The moose was near the lake, just where moose are supposed to be. Down low, either in riparian areas or lower meadows, were the deer. The elk ranged in and out of the aspen. The bighorn sheep worked their way across the high slopes, never far from the steeper "escape terrain" they depend upon for safety. The goats were above all the others, in their most photogenic habitat of nearly sheer rock walls. And in keeping with their legend, the grizzly bears showed up pretty much anywhere they wanted. It all had the ecological tidiness of a half-hour television nature show, lacking only a supremely confident commentator explaining how nicely all this habitat partitioning works.

And in fact, it does work well. It's hardly that simple in real life, but on average, what I saw that day provided a good overview of how these big animals divide up the park, spreading their populations and attention across the layers and levels of geology and vegetation to the best possible advantage.

APPETITES

We North Americans, even those of us with a special interest in nature, tend to see our wild country as inhabited by a small set of animals—nothing like the amazing diversity of Africa or southern Asia. Though we hardly ever say so, we think of our native wildlife as fairly simple—just a few species of predators and a few species of prey.

But consider just the mammalian predators in Waterton-Glacier. Starting down from the largest, they include grizzly bear, black bear, mountain lion, gray wolf, wolverine, coyote, lynx, bobcat, badger, otter, fisher, striped skunk, mink, marten, long-tailed weasel, short-tailed weasel, least weasel, and a variety of shrews and bats. If the number of different-size animals is any measure of diversity, this is hardly a depauperate natural system. Their typical poundage, in the same order, is 250, 200, 110, 90, 40, 35, 20, 20, 20, 15, 10, 8, 2, 2, then, from the weasels on down, various fractions of a pound, until we get to the shrews, which are various fractions of an ounce.

▲ *Elk*

If that set of numbers doesn't represent a full enough spectrum of ecological niches, keep in mind that a very large and hungry number of birds, fish, reptiles, amphibians, and insects are also out there filling in the gaps. Most of them stay anonymous to the average visitor, but they are not anonymous to each other.

▲ *Nuthatch*

When you think about the incredible number of combinations of predator and prey that exist among all these meat eaters and their even more diverse victims, you begin to doubt that even the term "web of life" does justice to the richness of what's going on out there. The intertwinings, interweavings, and interlockings are just too rich for the web metaphor. It's more like a tapestry of life, or a Persian rug of life. A large part of what is consumable is of interest to a large percentage of the consumers, who often seem limited only by how big a piece of someone else they can fit in their mouths. If it's too big to kill, they'll wait until something else kills it and then sneak up to the carcass for a quick snack.

On the other hand, almost all of them, from the largest grizzly bear to the smallest shrew, eat insects. These in turn chew or bite or otherwise live off the mammals while they are alive and feast on their carcasses when they're not. Studies elsewhere in the Rockies have revealed that several dozen species of highly specialized beetles make their entire living from large mammal carcasses; some of these beetles are so specialized they prey only on other beetles that scavenge only these carcasses. When you consider all the larger scavengers and the amazing number of invertebrates and smaller animals who help clean up a carcass, you realize that a dead elk is itself a very complex ecosystem.

We've learned a lot about how these large mammals interact, and perhaps the most striking thing we've learned is that life is hard. Between 1989 and 1994, thirty-two deer, twenty-three elk, and twelve moose, all females, were radio-collared in and near the park along the North Fork of the Flathead River. Of these sixty-seven ungulates, mountain lions killed ten deer and eleven elk. Wolves killed eight deer, three elk, and four moose. Bears killed two deer, three elk, and three moose. Coyotes killed four deer. Humans killed four deer, five elk, and two moose. Three deer, one elk, and two moose died of unknown causes, and one moose died from an accident. Only one

▼ *Bunny*

of the sixty-seven radio-collared animals, a deer, was known to have died from old age.

Predators' appetites know no professional courtesy either; they'll eagerly eat each other or each other's food. Wolf researchers discovered the remains of a mountain lion kitten that had been caught and killed by wolves and have documented wolves taking lions' kills away from them. A more recent addition to the local carnivore lore was a grizzly bear in northwestern Glacier Park in the 1990s who spent part of its winter out of its den making a comfortable living by chasing wolves away from their fresh kills (this behavior has the wonderful formal name "kleptoparasitism," a term that I am surprised has never been adopted by humans to describe some of their own kind). Opportunism is the word of the day.

▲ *Kootenai Lakes Lion Tracks*

INVISIBLE PREDATOR

Marsha and I were hiking into Avalanche Lake with our friends Helen Porter and Henry Shovic. We were in the densest, shadiest forest along the way—what I think of as Hansel and Gretel woods—when our eyes caught a quick, dark motion back among the trees to the right. As we watched, a small, chocolate brown animal—it looked like an overgrown weasel who had made himself a suit from my mother's old mink stole—came bounding along parallel to our route, making unbelievably easy jumps from downed log to rock to stump to ground. Though I see the winter tracks of this animal all the time, and occasionally see an actual individual, it still took me a minute to realize that I was looking at a marten, the personification of opportunistic appetite.

The American marten, until recently known as the pine marten, is a good example of the elegant complexity of a wilderness, in part because Glacier's martens have been fruitfully studied and so there's a lot known, in part because they're out there doing lots of interesting things without most people even knowing they exist, and in part because the marten offers some lessons in how overlapping and interwoven wild animals' lives are.

Perhaps the most detailed analysis of marten droppings done anywhere in North America took place in Glacier, conducted by two Montana Fish and Game Department biologists, Richard Weckwerth

Deer in Aspen

and Vernon Hawley. During a six-year period in the 1950s, Weckwerth and Hawley collected, disassembled, and identified the contents of 1,758 marten scats. What they found revealed just how much of a dietary generalist the marten is. Glacier's martens, with home ranges of less than a square mile among the males and about a quarter of a square mile among females, ate at least fifteen species of small mammals (voles, mice, lemmings, rabbits, and squirrels), several species of birds, insects from a variety of orders, at least twenty species of seeds, and a number of other interesting oddments, including bats and elk (the latter eaten as carrion; let's not give the marten *that* much credit).

Most visitors won't see even one, but there are lots of martens out there, and in winter their presence is always obvious in the snow, as they move from tree to tree, on the lookout for the unwary squirrel just as they keep their eyes open for carrion and anything else that may look appetizing. The one we saw along the trail to Avalanche Lake that day eased back into the anonymous forest as quickly as it appeared, leaving us grateful for the sighting but longing for a better acquaintance with such a mysterious little carnivore.

BULL

The farthest north, and most remote, of the long, narrow lakes up the west side of the park is Kintla. When you look north from Kintla Lake, you see Starvation Ridge and the Boundary Mountains and know that Canada is on the other side. The trail follows the north shore of the lake for six or seven miles, sometimes winding perversely away from the lakeshore and up over a steep hill, as if the trail crew decided that hikers should have to suffer a little to enjoy such a wonderful view.

▲ *American Marten*

My friend Steve Gniadek, mentioned earlier, has a priceless combination of qualities for a hiking companion: formidable biological knowledge, a good sense of humor, and a stoic, if not quite eager, willingness to carry the heavy stuff if I don't seem quite up to it (I never seem up to it, even when I probably am). He was also happy for an excuse to make a late fall trip up the Kintla drainage, past Kintla Lake to its smaller sister, Upper Kintla. Upper Kintla is if anything lovelier than Kintla, its shoreline uninterrupted by development or other signs of humans.

Bull Trout ▶

I was here especially to get a look at a bull trout, which spawn in small numbers in Kintla Creek just below the lake. Sean Meegan, a seasonal biological technician with the National Park Service at the time, was camped near the outlet and generously guided these unannounced guests to the best spot.

We had a lot to talk about on the short walk down the creek. Sean's camp had been visited by a lion the night before, and there were bear tracks along the creek. No doubt the bears wanted a look at the bull trout, too. Whenever I encounter backcountry researchers, rangers, and other people who get to spend extended periods away from the roads rather than just pass through, I am a little envious of that small subset of wilderness travelers for whom the backcountry becomes something more like a home. Sean was obviously having a big time doing his job.

As he was there to study the bull trout, he had no trouble putting us in the right spot. It turned out that the best spot for looking at them was on the other side of the creek, so Sean loaned me his chest waders. I went a little way downstream, waded quietly across the channel, climbed up on a gravel bar, put on my polaroids, and squinted into the bright water.

After a minute or two, I was able to pick out the shapes of several big trout, up to eighteen or twenty inches, as they moved slowly here and there in the deepest part of the green water of the pool. Their profiles were flattened by refraction, but there was no doubt about what they were. The leading edges of their pectoral and pelvic fins were so white they almost glowed. Like their near-relatives the brook and lake trout, bull trout have very pretty, multicolored underfins. For many years now, from the Everglades to Alaska, I have watched and photographed fish with the same enthusiasm that many people reserve for birds, so this was a pretty satisfying moment.

Since the 1980s the bull trout has become a powerful symbol for much of what has happened to wild aquatic ecosystems throughout the American West. It is illegal to kill one in the park, and Upper Kintla Lake contained the last large population of bull trout that had not had any non-native fishes dumped on top of it. Elsewhere in the bull trout's range in the West, introduced lake trout have hammered it, introduced brook trout have confused its genetics by breeding with it, and introduced fishermen have overharvested it. In 1998, not long after I watched the bull trout that day at the outlet of Upper Kintla Lake, the species was classified as threatened under the terms of the Endangered Species Act. A more recent study in Lake McDonald, where the native bull trout were disastrously reduced in numbers by introduced lake trout many years ago, suggests that it could be possible to give the bull trout in that lake a boost by selectively netting the lake trout when they're concentrated in shallower water during spawning season.

For all the damage they have admittedly sustained, national parks are still rightly viewed as among the last strongholds of a number of rare native fishes such as the bull trout. Like almost all western waters, Glacier's lakes and streams were long subjected to heavy stocking of a variety of non-native sport fish, six species of which took hold and now dominate many waters. Many fishless high-country lakes and ponds, representing unique aquatic plant and invertebrate communities, were arduously stocked by pack trains in the interest of improving the fishing for early visitors. The inadvertent result was the irrevocable alteration of whatever biological system had developed in those waters over the past ten thousand years. By the time all stocking ceased in 1972, massive changes had been inflicted on the native aquatic world here.

In 2004, celebrating the thirtieth anniversary of my first visit to Waterton-Glacier, Marsha and I made the short but steep hike to Bertha Lake, just a few miles from Waterton Townsite. It was mostly an outing for the beauty of the trail—we counted more than forty species of wildflowers and engaged in endless vista gawking—but I

*Mountain Lady's Slipper,
Bertha Lake Trailhead*

brought along a light fly rod and a small assortment of flies. While Marsha settled on the little beach and sketched the ridge that loomed to the northeast, I spent about twenty minutes in happy casting and landed two finely colored little rainbow trout.

They are unquestionably beautiful animals. And unlike the blister rust I mentioned in the previous chapter, we brought these rainbow trout here on purpose. To the average fisherman, the experience would have been nearly perfect, and to me it was mighty good. But after all these years of studying and thinking about the aesthetic and even moral consequences of what we've done in our attempts to "improve" wild landscapes, I never catch a non-native fish without a certain regret. We have never really improved any wild landscape, and certainly we don't do so by dumping strange new life forms on it, however beautiful or extraordinary they may be in their own right.

I cannot bury my mixed feelings in any long-haul perspective on the inevitability of changing landscapes. The rainbow trout, a Pacific-drainage fish, has no ecological business in a place like this, any more than do the equally beautiful eastern brook trout I caught not long after, a couple of drainages to the north, from Crandell Lake. It isn't about beauty, or sport; it's about belonging or not belonging. It's about the pricelessness of authenticity we find in unmanipulated nature. It's about the humility of accepting nature on the terms it offers rather than succumbing to the arrogance of thinking we can always fix things even if they show no evidence of being broken. If humans had stayed away from Bertha Lake for another twenty thousand years, the rainbow trout would not have come there on its own.

▲ *Bertha Lake Rainbow*

But for all the compromises we've inflicted on it, these parks' waters are still important reservoirs of native fishes. Besides protecting bull trout, Glacier remains one of the last strongholds of lake populations of westslope cutthroat trout. Almost everywhere else, introductions of rainbow, brown, and even other types of cutthroats have outcompeted the native westslope cutthroats.

Fish have a lot to teach us in places like this, and they pay a heavy price for the lessons we learn. We only faintly understand what we set in motion when we tinker with these systems. In the end, our actions always bite back.

▲ Bald Eagle

THE EAGLE AND THE SHRIMP

An especially helpful and yet vexing example of the twisted course of such aquatic tinkering is the story of the kokanee salmon of McDonald Creek. It is the kind of story that chills the hearts and heats the conversations of all of us who seek to understand just what national parks offer us and how they should be managed. Ultimately it is not a story of fish but of an entire sprawling ecosystem and how one unforesightful action echoes through it forever.

Flathead Lake, southwest of Glacier National Park, has been a regionally important sport fishery for more than a century. Lake trout and kokanee salmon were both introduced there about a century ago, and they soon replaced the native westslope cutthroat trout. As Glacier's west-side rivers generally drain into the Flathead drainage, lake trout and kokanee salmon had access to many park waters. By the 1930s, the kokanee, who were stream spawners (lake trout spawn in lakes) found their way up from Flathead Lake into the Flathead River and into Glacier National Park, where they discovered excellent spawning habitat in McDonald Creek, just below Lake McDonald. Here they spawned by the thousands, and, like all Pacific salmon, died as soon as they were done.

Scavengers noticed this abundance of fish right away. In 1939, 37 bald eagles were counted along this little stretch of water, and that number grew to what has been called "the densest concentration of the species south of Canada." In 1981, when more than 100,000 kokanee entered the stream to spawn, the eagle count was 639. People flocked to see them. Photographers and the magazines that published their glorious art reduced the scene to a beautiful cliché—whether you were ever there or not, if you read many nature magazines in those days, you saw these breathtaking photographs. A single bald eagle is almost too much beauty and wonder to bear; to see dozens at once, even in photographs, brought on a kind of giddy emotional overload.

I lived in Wyoming and southern Montana through much of the 1970s and 1980s, so I often heard about this eagle show, and I always meant to go see it. I shouldn't have waited.

Starting in the late 1960s, the state of Montana introduced a non-native crustacean, opossum shrimp, into some lakes in the upper Flathead River Valley. The idea was that these shrimp would serve as a food that was expected to accelerate the growth of sport fish. By 1981, the shrimp had been washed downstream to Flathead Lake, and something went spectacularly wrong. The kokanee population collapsed with almost incredible swiftness. In 1987, only 330 kokanee entered McDonald Creek, and in 1989 only 50 showed up. The eagles didn't hang around to see what humans would come up with next, and the show was over.

What went wrong was typically, almost elegantly, complex. The kokanee in Flathead Lake were unable to feed on the shrimp because the two species' habits placed them at different depths at all the opportune times. Perhaps worse, the shrimp turned out to be extraordinarily effective predators on the lake's zooplankton (especially water fleas), which also happened to be the most important prey for the kokanee; the shrimp outcompeted the kokanee for this all-important food source, and the kokanee population plunged. At the same time, lake trout did well; apparently the juvenile lake trout were much better positioned to feed heavily on the shrimp, and as the lake trout grew bigger they seem to have become more effective predators on the kokanee, too.

There are engaging ironies in the disappointment this all caused. Here was a national park with a terrific wildlife attraction—not only a sensational salmon run but also a remarkable gathering of predators and scavengers, including eagles, bears, coyotes, otters, mink, gulls, and ducks. But the whole thing was based on the intrusion into the ecosystem of a non-native animal, an introduced fish. By almost any of the prevailing definitions of national parks, the show was "unnatural." But it was also wildly popular, and among the Waterton-Glacier visitors and locals who reminisce about it, one rarely hears any sentiments of relief that the native ecosystem has been to some extent restored. And considering our ongoing concern about the well-being of many of those very predators and scavengers, it's easy to regret this loss, however artificial its circumstances. The park's "unnatural" situation was without question benefiting the regional bald eagle population, and that has to have been a good thing. Nobody ever said managing national parks was going to be simple.

Nobody ever said any of these stories would ever truly end either. In the few years up to and including 2008, a small spawning run (at times at least a few hundred) of kokanee salmon has caused some local stir, this time coming up from Lake McDonald into McDonald Creek above the lake and near the mouth of Snyder Creek (near the Avalanche Lake trailhead). Apparently some age classes of Lake McDonald's lingering kokanee population have escaped predation by the lake trout to a great enough extent to become a modest but noticeable spectacle again.

COMEBACK

Gray Wolf

Not all modern wildlife stories are about losses. Sometimes we get organized, search our souls for a higher vision, and do something right. Or, just as good, we let nature go ahead and do something right on our behalf. Among the more troubling legacies of the "Old West" was the destruction of some of the most interesting animals of the wilderness, the predators. Gray wolves were essentially eliminated from the Northern Rockies in the United States by the early 1900s, when people believed that the line between good and bad animals was a very simple one. This story has been told often, perhaps most eloquently by Barry Lopez in his classic *Of Wolves and Men* (1978) but by many, many other writers and biologists as well. David Mech, the world's foremost wolf scientist and wolf conservation advocate, has written a superb set of books about wolves that will introduce you to the world of the wolf with an informational depth that was simply unimaginable thirty years ago. Lopez, Mech, and many others have given us a real wolf to moderate—I'd like to say replace, but that's asking for too much—the sensational, unforgettable, and often tragic myths we cherished and nurtured for so many centuries.

The fear of the planet's nonhuman carnivores and omnivores has led us humans to behavior that is little less cruel and foolish than our worst treatment of each other. But times change, and so do attitudes. Though quite a few westerners, including many of those in political power, still fear or hate wolves, public surveys suggest that the vast majority of the American public now takes a more tolerant and affirmative view. Since the early 1990s, wolf recovery in the western United States has become, in the words of biologist John Varley (who oversaw Yellowstone's wolf recovery program through its critical first decade), a "growth industry."

Since the early 1980s, wolves from southern Canada have ranged farther and farther into Montana. By 1993, there were three packs that included some part of Glacier National Park in their territories. Other packs and individuals explored other areas in Montana, so that by 1995 the Montana wolf population was perhaps seventy animals. That same year, after more than half a century with very few or no wolves, Yellowstone National Park received its first introductions of new wolves (flown in from Canada), which have thrived in the region's prey-rich ecosystem, setting off a whole new round of debate over the effects of wolf predation on regional ungulate populations. In 2008, wolves were well enough reestablished in Montana, Idaho, and Wyoming to be officially removed from the Endangered Species List in the lower forty-eight states, but ensuing lawsuits and a change in presidential administrations resulted in their return to the list in early 2009. Recent estimates place the number of wolves in Glacier at around fifty.

With the wolves come further changes in public attitudes. Now that the wolves have been around for a while and the dire predictions of massive livestock slaughter and routine attacks on humans have been shown to be unfounded, tolerance has increased. Commerce hasn't hurt the wolf either, as wolf-related gifts, clothing, art, and other items are stocked abundantly in stores around the park and the state. Though the mystique of the wolf has clearly captured the hearts of a great many people, there is still intense disapproval of wolves, especially of their effects on the big game animals that we have always been unwilling to share with them. The full social, ecological, and political consequences of wolf recovery remain difficult to predict, but wolves seem pretty well established as a new part of the New West.

In Waterton-Glacier, as I've already explained, the wolf joined many other predator species, all determined to make a living on the available prey species. The wolf did not wander into a predator-exempt system but into a very busy neighborhood where making a living is hard work.

If you're lucky, you'll see some sign of a wolf. If you're really lucky, perhaps you'll see the animal itself. And if you are most lucky of all, you

Downhill Grizzly ▶

will hear their howls. The Waterton-Glacier country has been healed a little by this colonization of a lost native, and the experience of the park is enriched by their presence, even if that experience does not include a sighting.

GRIZZLY NEWS

It is especially appropriate that Andy Russell's book, *Grizzly Country* (1967), a classic account of the North American grizzly bear and its world—and an eloquent plea for the conservation of that world—opened with his tale of a pack trip into bear country in Waterton Lakes National Park. It is thanks almost entirely to a few national parks in the western United States that the grizzly bear survived at all in the lower forty-eight states. The same early national park managers who so efficiently finished off the last wolves in the great western parks in the early 1900s saw something worth saving in the bears and let them survive. Though they are also wild carnivores, bears matter to us in ways wolves never have. Countless human cultures have made a special and very complicated place for bears in their hearts. The national parks have contributed enormously to the meaning and symbolism of bears in American society.

This is not to say that our dealings with grizzly bears have been easy, even in the parks. My own first awareness of the bears of Glacier National Park dates to the same year Russell's wonderful book was published, when as a college student I read a far less uplifting, indeed terrifying, article about two young women killed in different locations by different bears in the park on the same night. As an indication of how divorced Americans had become from the reality and value of wilderness life, those tragic deaths led to sincere and forceful calls for the immediate extermination of all grizzly bears from American parks.

Fortunately, wiser heads eventually prevailed. We got to keep the bears, and, in good part in response to the lessons of the 1967 Glacier tragedies, the craft of bear management was set on a course of professionalization that enabled it to better confront the real risks of having such powerful animals around. Our life with grizzly bears will always be exciting and deeply rewarding, but it will never be simple.

Like wolves, grizzly bears were long regarded as little less than evil demons by enough westerners that between the late 1800s and mid-1900s the bears were exterminated from almost all of their habitats in Mexico and the United States south of Canada. Despite the heartfelt appeals of Russell and many other conservationists, as recently as ten years ago it still seemed to many of us that the survival of the grizzly bear in the lower forty-eight states was in doubt.

Things have gotten a little better now. There is a cautiously optimistic mood among most grizzly bear managers in the American West.

We have turned a corner, the public is increasingly engaged and determined to save the grizzly bear, and bear numbers have increased in their various remaining lower forty-eight habitats. Best of all, it's now clear that we have the tools and skills to keep them around, and there are persistent calls for reestablishing them in long-vacant grizzly bear habitats elsewhere in the West. Considering the intense and relentless pressures of development and human population growth in and near grizzly country, there is no room for complacency, but there is more room for hope than there has been for many years.

The colorful and often sad history of the grizzly bear in the United States makes a recent research project in the Glacier area all the more exciting. In nearly a century since the park's establishment, the bears had remained uncounted—an uncertainty that made conservationists nervous, because without that basic information, there was no way to know if the population was thriving or in trouble. But between 2003 and 2008, a team of researchers under the leadership of Kate Kendall (mentioned in chapter 3 for her work on whitebark pine), gathered grizzly bear hair samples for DNA analysis in order to create an up-to-the-year portrait of the grizzly bear population.

▲ *Bear Hair Snare*

Though certainly deserving of great public attention and acclaim as a milestone scientific work, this study probably owes much of its notoriety to two other, quite nonscientific factors. First, the popular mystery novelist Nevada Barr set one of her books, *Blood Lure* (2001), in Glacier, where Barr's always appealing ranger-sleuth, Anna Pigeon, finds herself helping out with an early stage of the hair-gathering project when a gruesome murder intrudes. Second, and rather less entertaining, for several years up to and including his 2008 presidential campaign, Republican candidate John McCain repeatedly singled out this study as what he regarded as an outrageous example of pork-barrel funding. I can only guess that McCain was receiving bad information and advice on this one, as all he accomplished by his complaining was to prove that even an authentic American hero sometimes gets it sadly wrong.

Because the grizzly bear in the United States had been classified as threatened under the terms of the Endangered Species Act in 1975, federal bear managers were legally responsible for determining the status of the population. Expensive long-term radio-collaring of grizzly bears in the Yellowstone National Park area starting fifty years ago has given managers there an excellent idea of that population's condition, but far less was known about the bears of the 7.8-million-acre area known as the Northern Continental Divide Ecosystem (NCDE), which runs from just north of Missoula, Montana, to the boundary between Glacier and Waterton Lakes National Parks. Kate's study provided that information and proved itself a remarkably nonintrusive and economical way to gather definitive information on a wildlife population.

The team of researchers created simple "hair traps" throughout key backcountry areas of the NCDE, using baited sites in which a strongly scented lure (Nevada Barr's "blood lure") was encircled by a strand of barbed wire run (usually strung between convenient trees near the lure) around it. Bears attracted to the scent had to crawl under or over the wire to get to the lure (they received no food "reward" for their effort), and thus unwittingly contributed a few hairs to the barbs. Researchers also identified trees that bears were known to favor for rubbing and attached short strips of barbed wire to those, too (bears apparently approved of the additional scratchiness provided by the barbed wire).

Immense amounts of time were spent dutifully preparing these little traps and monitoring them to collect the hair of all the bears who investigated them. By 2008, some 34,000 hair samples had been collected and analyzed, and the team arrived at an estimate of 765 grizzly bears in the NCDE. This is more than twice the number of bears that experts thought were there and indicates a robust and genetically vigorous population.

Still, we don't dare relax about grizzly bears. In fact, knowing just how many bears are there is all the more reason to ensure that their numbers don't decline into less comfortable levels. Only a fool—or someone with no knowledge of the history of the American West—could fail to notice that exactly the same economic and development pressures that exterminated grizzly bears from virtually all of their range in the United States are intensifying near these last few remaining strongholds. It makes so much more sense to protect the bears now rather than watch while they lose any more of their country. Conservationists have learned that it is infinitely harder and more expensive to restore a population of wild animals than it is to maintain it. We still have the chance here, in and around Waterton-Glacier, to get it right and keep the grizzly bear where it belongs, and where it can continue to be, in the words of Andy Russell, "the living symbol of the mountain wilderness."

THE SCATTERED SYSTEM

In the summer of 1983, when I was living in Livingston, Montana, I visited Glacier to interview then-Superintendent Bob Haraden as part of an assignment for *Newsweek*. Bob and I were friends from the 1970s, when he was assistant superintendent in Yellowstone and I was a grunt seasonal ranger-naturalist there, so it was easy to talk. I admired him for all his good work, and he was just then earning hero status among National Park Service people for standing up to the anti-environmentalism of Secretary of the Interior James Watt.

During our conversation, Bob summed up both the power and the powerlessness of trying to manage and protect a place that is so connected to the lands around it:

> There are damages we can stop, problems that, if we had enough rangers to line them up at arm's length all along the boundary, we could solve. But even if the rangers were twelve deep, they couldn't stop the acid rain from falling.

▲ *Blue Grouse*

What we have learned, in our approximately 130 years of experimenting with national parks, is that the boundaries don't work very well. They might be fine for the pine marten, with its tiny home range. They might even be fine for most of the park's animals and plants. Waterton-Glacier will continue to be a breathtaking place no matter what care we take of its neighboring lands. But it's good not to forget what is at stake, and a few examples should serve to make the point that these parks are no more an island than anyplace else on the planet. As Douglas Houston, an ecologist friend of mine puts it, "ecosystems leak."

The original creators of Glacier National Park thought primarily of preserving spectacular scenery, so it was relatively simple for them to draw lines on the map around the grandest mountains and call the result a national park. But even in 1910 there were forward-looking people who recognized that even parks as large as Glacier, or Yellowstone to the south, did not encompass nature's sprawling life communities completely. Much of the time it was wildlife, whether large herds of migratory herbivores or the carnivores that followed them, that compelled us to rethink the very idea of protecting natural areas.

In recent years we have reperceived these Rocky Mountain land-scapes on a series of progressively larger and more ambitious scales. I have already suggested the extent to which modern conservation-ists in the United States have responded to this problem by defining a larger area around Glacier National Park as special. The identification of the Northern Continental Divide Ecosystem—which includes all of Waterton-Glacier, the Bob Marshall-Great Bear-Scapegoat Wilderness complex to the south, and various other bordering lands—was driven in good part by the need to conserve grizzly bears and their habitats. The 7.8-million-acre NCDE, like the Greater Yellowstone Ecosystem to the south and other smaller areas in Montana, Idaho, and Washington, was defined to help empower management and conservation of grizzly bears in the United States. It honors the ecological realities of remain-ing grizzly bear habitat in the Northern Rockies but ends abruptly at the international boundary, north of which our Canadian friends take up the same responsibilities in their own ways.

The next step up is the Crown of the Continent Ecosystem (CCE), which formalizes recognition of the continuity of the biological setting by extending the NCDE into Canada as far as the southern end of Banff National Park for a total area of about 10.8 million acres. I like to think that George Bird Grinnell, who first popularized the term "Crown of the Continent" even before Waterton or Glacier became parks, would be pleased if not impressed to see this expansion of the concept.

▲ *Army Cutworm Moth*

The grandest step up is the last one. Known generally as the Yellowstone-to-Yukon (often abbreviated as Y2Y), this initiative identifies the entire two-thousand-mile assemblage of wild country and human communities from the Greater Yellowstone Ecosystem in Wyoming to the British Columbia-Yukon Territory boundary as a unified place whose natural heritage deserves special recognition and care.

I find only good things in all this big-picture thinking. I am grateful for the world's admiration for, and interest in, Waterton-Glacier. None of the recent redrawings of the regional map and none of the world honors that the parks have been given in any way compromise the authority of the American and Canadian people to manage their lands as they see fit. Reimagining these lands on a larger scale, whether as a contiguous set of wildlands that cross one international boundary or as places of planetary significance, can do us and our neighbors a lot of good. Specifically, they remind us of important ways the parks serve us. To understand this urge among conservationists to think big in the Northern Rockies, you only have to look at Waterton-Glacier and see how profoundly the life community in these places has always been tied to the lands around them.

Bison, which now survive in the parks only in a small captive herd near Waterton Townsite, once ranged the low country on the east side of both parks (I suppose some were on the west side, too). Early white accounts of the area mention many bones and skulls found in the lower valleys of the park. Some bison may have wintered in the more sheltered valleys in the park, while others may have moved long distances as part of the migratory tides of the great herds of the northern plains. By their migrations, these bison also defined a much larger ecosystem but one that extended far out onto the prairies rather than along the mountain ranges of the NCDC, CCE, and Y2Y. Caribou apparently also once inhabited portions of the northwestern corner of the park and perhaps other parts of the park. They're gone, and their migrations no longer enrich the ecological interconnections of this region.

But many other such wild travelers are still around and have the power to surprise us. A most unlikely and important migrant is the army cutworm moth. From mid- to late summer, all up and down the mountain ranges in and near Waterton-Glacier, some grizzly bears move to high-elevation talus slopes to eat these little moths. At their peak condition, these insects are more than half fat, almost a calorie each. They are at times superabundant, and heavy concentrations of them may hold bears in one area for several weeks. The moths are only there seasonally, having migrated to the high country from neighboring prairies.

Longer-distance fliers include the bald eagles that stopped over at McDonald Creek back when the kokanee were so abundant. Those birds were moving along a two-thousand-mile migration flyway that extends from their summering areas in the Mackenzie River Basin of far northern Canada to wintering areas in the United States, as far south as southern Utah.

Less celebrated but no less significant are all the little neotropical migrants: songbirds that summer in the Northern Rockies and winter in Central and South America, several thousand miles away. These, even more than the moths and eagles, are in grave danger, as their seasonal habitats are being destroyed in places that Bob Haraden's line of rangers may never have heard of.

The scale of these interconnections that tie Waterton-Glacier to faraway places is daunting and far beyond anything imagined by even the most ambitious early advocates of national parks in the United States and Canada. The parks are really only a tiny part of a vast and unappreciated Western Hemisphere Ecosystem, and it can only retain its ecological integrity if the rest of the planet does.

But it may be that the best part of this story is still to come, as we learn to listen to what the parks have to tell us not merely about their future but about ours. There are good reasons why national parks all over the world are now regarded as superb barometers of planetary health. They allow us to measure changes in those few natural systems—even if they are just small fragments of formerly continent-size systems—that have not been severely compromised by human action. Ever since the beginning of the national park movement in North America in the late 1800s, a few foresighted people have recognized the many boundary-crossing gifts these preserves give human society—gifts we now term "ecosystem services." Grinnell and his fellow pioneer conservationists had more than an inkling of the significance of these services; whether they were campaigning for the protection of New York's Adirondack Mountains or some wilderness area in the American West, they emphasized the value of these places as "reservoirs"—of wildlife, of wildness, and of resources of urgent practical value to human society. They constantly reminded us, for example, that protecting headwater river systems was just good sense for the sake of agriculture downstream, and there was no better way to protect those headwaters than by placing them under the protection of national parks like Glacier.

We have more recently learned better how to measure the extent of these ecosystem services. Vanishing glaciers, shifting plant and wildlife populations, shrinking rivers, and other startling features of the landscape of today's Northern Rockies suggest nature's restlessness under our increasing impact and make Waterton-Glacier an unexcelled classroom for examining our own future.

CHAPTER FOUR

Three Cirques

NOTES FROM THE GREAT DIVIDE

RISERS

About dusk, small rainbow trout began rising here and there thirty or forty yards out from the lakeshore. I much prefer stream fishing to lake fishing (it would amaze the uninitiated how snooty fly fishermen can be about where they'll bother to fish, even with feeding trout in sight), but I'd brought a rod and a "light vest" (read: a vest with only a few hundred flies in it), so I knew I should give it a try.

On a stream, I'll usually bother to study the situation a little, but on a lake I just tie on some general, hopeful, big fly and start slapping it out there, wishing for this to be a night the fish don't care what I offer. What the hell, they're just little rainbows in a wilderness lake; how smart can they be, right?

77

It's my fate that they usually do care, and they can be very smart. On this evening, my line had a heavy leader, but I didn't want to bother putting on a finer one that would be less obvious to the fish, so I sloshed out into the shallows and started casting.

It was immediately clear that I needed much more than the right fly. What I really needed was chest waders, preferably insulated ones, or even a boat. I was wading in shorts, and this water was *cold*. Besides, I'd borrowed Marsha's rubber sandals, which were about three inches too short for my feet; my heels overhung them and kept coming down on sharp rocks, so I accompanied my casting with a refrain of "Ooch, ouch, ooch" as I waded along. Worst of all, every time I laid that heavy leader and big fly out over a riser, the terrified trout immediately fled the area.

For a while I thought that my only consolation would be the glorious view. Steep ridges with dark, twisted strata ran up in various directions, towering more than two thousand feet above the lake on three sides, and were reflected hugely in the still water. But then, as so often happens when I start fishing lazily and without thought, I became engaged in the game. Up to my waist and shivering in the cold lake, I used what was left of the light to improve my gear, experimenting with smaller and smaller flies, tiptoeing into deeper spots to make longer and more delicate casts over the elusive little risers.

▼ *Wet Fly*

Just as my feet began to go numb and it got too dark to pick another fly from the box, I attached a three-foot section of very fine tippet material to my leader, tied on a tiny Quill Gordon (a #20, for you fishermen) and put it over another riser. The fish rose confidently, took it, and was hooked. Uttering a loud and triumphant "Ha!" I hauled back on the rod like a tuna fisherman landing an eighty-pounder, the leader parted like spider web, and my fish was gone.

It is another part of fly fishing's odd reward system that one can feel so successful without landing a fish. Having now figured out the situation and having proven it by hooking a trout, I didn't need to continue. I made a few more hopeful casts but soon returned to the tent in search of some warm socks and maybe a little wine.

MODERN CAMPING

The most pronounced difference I've noticed between Glacier and other places I've hiked is that in Glacier, designated backcountry campsites are not strung out along the trail at discrete distances from one another. Instead, the Glacier backcountry campsites are clustered in small campgrounds. Each of these campgrounds has one small area designated for food preparation and eating, and that is the only place you are supposed to have food with you. If you're not actively involved in preparing and eating your food, it should be hanging from the appropriate food storage cable, strung high between two trees some distance from the campground.

There are typically four or five campsites nearby. When you arrive at the campground, you find the site that your permit entitles you to and make yourself at home. In my experience, the sites are usually tucked into enough cover that the other sites may not be visible at all, but even at that, the effect of such camping is quite different from having your own little piece of the wilderness to yourself.

I don't doubt the wisdom of the system. Each park has to arrange its sites to suit the landscape, and in Glacier's setting I can readily appreciate the value of concentrating use this way (by contrast, in Alaska's Denali National Park, except near some developments, there aren't even designated trails, much less campsites; in the very different Denali vegetation, it makes most sense to disperse the foot traffic and camping impacts as randomly as possible across the whole landscape).

Where the complications accrue most rapidly is in that small cooking-and-eating space, which you share with members of the parties camped at the other campsites. There, whether you want to or not, you are a social person in a social setting. For me, it's a little too much like all those lovely bed-and-breakfasts where you come down in the morning hoping for a quiet cup of coffee but knowing that you're at risk of landing next to a sharp-voiced insurance salesman, two weeks out of Duluth and desperate for some dialogue on the issues of the day. Breakfast isn't a meal I like to have to brace myself for.

Most of the time, though, you meet nice people and it's fun, but here at Gunsight Lake it was sad. In the center of the dining area, a slight, middle-aged woman was stationed, and throughout our cooking, eating, and cleanup she kept up a constant and nearly manic "conversation" with whomever would make eye contact. We tried to do our share in acknowledging her presence and need, but our little responses felt hopeless, even unnecessary, in the face of her urgent ramblings.

▲ *Hanging the Panniers*

Miles

It quickly became clear that she was authentically troubled. In our party, Wendy, a nurse by profession, wondered if this poor soul had been unwisely released from medication. We were left to conclude that her hiking partner had parked her here for others to tend to for a little while so he could retreat to his tent for a few moments of silence. It was such an awkward, sorrowful, and unusual situation that I simply couldn't decide what might be the kindest thing to do. So I also retreated as soon as I could.

GUNSIGHT GOATS

Gunsight Lake occupies a mile-long trough at the bottom of a more or less east-facing cirque that drains northeast from the park and eventually into Hudson Bay. From the lake it's a three-mile climb and a two-thousand-foot elevation change to Gunsight Pass and the Continental Divide. There were nine of us in the group: Marsha and I in one tent; Jeremy, Wendy, and their two-year-old daughter, Kestrel, in another tent; and Miles, Zerc, Pinball, and Petey, our rent-a-llamas, over by the hitching post. We'd made the six-mile hike in from the Going-to-the-Sun Road that day, and while I fished that evening, the others tidied up the cooking gear, hung our bright red llama panniers to keep them out of reach of bears and deer, and generally got comfortable for the night.

There were some big fires west of the park—it was so dry that the national forests out that way were closed to hiking. But for us, high in the park, the only effect of the fires was to make all the views hazy and the predawn skies a deep rose. On such a dawn, after two cool nights camped at the shore of this lake, we rammed everything back in the panniers, hung them on the sides of the llamas, and marched off to conquer the pass. After the rest of us crossed the swaying footbridge across the outlet of the lake, Marsha (wearing her own sandals now) led the "pack string" of four llamas across the shallow stream, and we began to climb.

I'd never before encountered an animal who seemed to get so absorbed in a good view the way the llamas did. Whenever we stopped at a steep place, "my" llama, Miles, would move right to the edge and gaze intently off into the smoky distance. I suppose a few thousand generations of South American mountain lions made him that way, but it was fun to pretend that he was as impressed by the view as we were.

They were terrific animals to hike with. They were cooperative, attentive, and enormously amusing, and their habit of humming back and forth to each other was a soothing force I missed for weeks after the trip was over. It only took them a day or so to have the rest of us quietly humming, now and then, in imitation or just because it felt good.

But the llamas weren't prepared for goats. This was all the more surprising because they barely deigned to notice the deer we encountered on the trail and at the Gunsight Lake campsite.

Gunsight Pass's goats, a little like the goats at Logan Pass on the Going-to-the-Sun Road, were famous. Because of their habituation to people (which makes them both a management problem and easy to study), they've been the subject of repeated research projects, and we'd been assured we'd have no trouble seeing them. We didn't.

Sad to say, neither did the llamas. We'd stopped for a snack-and-water break about three quarters of the way to the pass when Miles and Zerc, the two lead llamas, became intent on a distant white object high on the slope above us. Zerc suddenly let loose with the llama's alarm call, a sound much like a turkey would make if it weighed about four hundred pounds. It was a sound so loud that you don't want to be standing directly by the llama's mouth (as Marsha was) when he makes it. The goat eventually disappeared behind a low ridge, so we stowed our water bottles and headed on up the trail. I was leading Miles. Marsha was right behind me with Zerc, followed by Wendy leading Pinball and Petey strung together.

A minute later, I led Miles around a sharp turn in the trail and was suddenly confronted with a nanny and kid goat only twenty feet away. Miles bolted in a panic, leaving the trail and scrambling back downhill across a steep rocky meadow, dragging panniers, packs, and—until I had the good sense to let go of his rope—me. Though I was too busy to notice, Zerc had done the same thing, but Marsha had the good sense to let go right away.

At first I feared that the llamas were planning to retreat way down the mountain. I was at least grateful that this encounter hadn't happened on one of the narrow places where the only choices were back down the trail or over the edge. But we soon realized that all they

Llamas on a Rope ▶

wanted to do was get together. As soon as all four were standing side by side facing the perceived threat, they were, well, perhaps not okay but at least willing to stand still.

It took a while to resolve this situation. We had to hold the llama's reins very tight while the two goats bypassed us by skirting across another meadow so they could move down the trail, but eventually we were able to restore Miles's panniers, make sure none of us had broken anything (Miles was only bleeding a little from one leg, and my twisted ankle hardly hurt at all), and move on. From then on, for the next couple of days, whenever we were hiking a steep, winding trail, I could look back and see all four llamas craning their necks as far out to one side as possible, to see what sort of bizarre surprise we might spring on them next.

Much more than the grizzly bear, the mountain goat has been the traditional symbol of Glacier National Park. The Great Northern Railway, which had so much to do with the opening of Glacier to visitors in its early years, adopted the goat as its symbol, and a more admirable one is hard to imagine. Goats are easily seen from a number of roadside locations and are great fun to watch with binoculars or spotting scopes. Once you see them in action on a steep mountainside (rather than slurping up tasty radiator antifreeze in the parking lot at Logan Pass), you'll immediately appreciate why they inspire such awe. A band of goats picking its way across a nearly sheer cliff face can inspire as much disbelief as empathetic nervousness. In his fascinating book, *A Beast the Color of Winter: The*

Mountain Goat Observed (1983), ecologist Douglas Chadwick described how the goat's exceptional traction and tremendous chest and shoulder muscles allow it to move around:

> I have seen mountain goats perform what amounted to one-handed chin-ups. Having only a scrap of momentum behind them they reached out, hooked one hoof on an overhead shelf, and hauled themselves up by it alone.

So, while it's wonderful to see one along a road, the real treat is seeing one, even at a great distance, on one of the high steep places they make their home.

A two-thousand-foot pass isn't that hard a climb if a llama is carrying all your gear, and we enjoyed a leisurely lunch by the stone shelter house at Gunsight Pass, letting the stiff breeze dry us off as we absorbed

▼ *Lake Ellen Wilson*

both the view and the idea of being on the Continental Divide. From now on, all the water we saw would be draining to the Flathead Valley, the Columbia River, and the Pacific Ocean. Looking west down from the pass, we could see our next destination, Lake Ellen Wilson, about a thousand feet lower and a couple of miles by trail away.

All the way down, the llamas, especially Zerc, scanned the nearby hillsides nervously. Zerc occasionally blasted another alarm call into Marsha's ear just to make sure we didn't spend too much time stopping to enjoy the long, flower-bordered cascades that tumbled from snowfields and glacial remnants on the slopes of Mount Jackson to our south. It worked; Marsha, surly and nearing deafness in one ear, insisted we keep moving until we were at the lake.

But that evening the goats abandoned their highlands and joined us in camp. Habituated to people by several decades of foot traffic, the Gunsight goats spent their nights right in the camping area, where they sought out the salt left where people and livestock have urinated, or the sweet taste of toothpaste spit on the vegetation (they've even been known to lick sweat from the arms and legs of hikers, but we didn't get that cozy with them). This familiarity, both charming and dismaying, at least allowed me to get some close-up photographs of goats, but when I looked at them later, they all seemed unreal; my mind kept telling me that goats that close must be taxidermic mounts. Who would believe that a wild animal would let people get so close?

All night, these animals that I've always admired as a great symbol of remote and untouchable wildness brushed past our tents, clambered around on boulders, and repeatedly approached the llamas. I don't think Zerc slept at all; every hour or so during the night, I'd hear him cut loose again, and I'd drift off wondering if the other llamas wished he'd shut up, too.

REPOSE

It rained during the night. Between that and Zerc's hourly goat reports, I probably didn't sleep much better than he did, but I was more or less asleep at about five when I was roused by distant thunder. At first I thought we were in for a bigger storm, but then I recognized the noise as the roar of an avalanche somewhere out along the cirque. It occurred to me for about the thousandth time that nature keeps being nature all night long, even when we sack out and stop paying attention. Gravity never forgets.

Next morning, it was Jeremy who visually located the slide. When we arrived the day before, we'd noticed a small glacial trough on the steep slopes along the south shore of the lake opposite our campsite— a place where a small glacier had carved a narrow path through the rock, with its terminal moraines down

▲ *Junco*

close to the lakeshore. The long, slanting snow-and-ice field that covered the bottom of this trough may or may not have been what was left of the glacier. At the head of the trough perched a pile of big boulders and car-sized chunks of ice. During the night, this stuff, many tons of it, finally surrendered to the heat of summer and broke free. It crashed and slid the length of the ice field, leaving a series of straight white scars on the old gray snow, rolled through the opening between the two terminal moraines, and came to rest in a scatter on the lowest slopes. It all seemed a little distant in the morning light, like a model train layout, but remembering the power of its thunder, I realized it would have been a terrifying, exhilarating thing to witness while standing on one of those moraines.

INTRUSIONS

We enjoyed our camp at Lake Ellen Wilson. When nature is as generous as this, you simply don't notice the little problems, though I will admit that when they come to mind now, long after the trip is over, they seem formidable enough. The open-air pit toilet, which was tastefully located a short hike from the small group of campsites, afforded the contemplative user an unparalleled view of the surrounding mountains but had a perilously tilted seat, which made any involvement with it problematic. The failures of previous users' trajectories were so abundant that we were not in the least encouraged to try to straighten the seat.

Though the neighborhood goats were beautiful and photogenic beyond all reason, having so many of those stiletto-headed wild mammals wandering by just a few feet away was actually a little scary. The lake was too cold for wading or swimming and showed no promise for fishing. But, as I say, none of this mattered much because of the relentless swamping of our senses by all the beauty. What did matter was one appalling little episode of unnecessary violence to the setting, when a helicopter came near our cirque.

The magnitude and damage of the excursion helicopter in a wilderness setting is almost certainly not known to the customers who choose to hire the things. I like to think that most people, if they knew how utterly they were wrecking someone else's experience of the park, would have the decency not to do it. But I realize that may be naive. For all too many people, wilderness is just another commodified destination, not all that clearly defined beyond the conviction of their personal right to some imagined share of it.

It began rather abruptly. There was the ominous thwop-thwop-thwop of the approaching aircraft, then it entered some neighboring cirque and suddenly became a profoundly obnoxious roar that lasted for several minutes. We never actually saw the helicopter. The sound seemed to come from all over the sky and rattle down into our cirque like hell's own echo.

I realize that I can't even say for certain that it wasn't a government helicopter, surveying wildlife or rescuing a climber (not that ownership of the machine has much effect on how annoying it is). But based on what I know about such air traffic in parks, I feel safe assuming it was a tourist flight. It hung around up there just out of sight, thwopping a mighty racket down on us so the pilot could give the passengers the requisite cheap thrill of whatever spectacular and completely unearned view they were enjoying.

Then it faded and was gone, though it echoed through our silence-conditioned brains for a long time. We wondered if maybe it was over the pass toward Gunsight Lake, but it's more likely that it was somewhere above Sperry Glacier, to our north. Sound pollution is an ongoing hot issue in national park management, and you only have to encounter this particular pollutant once to understand why. It is an unkind act, made no less so by the apparent ignorance of those committing it.

PREDATORS AT LAST

We got an earlier start the next morning, having ten miles between us and the next cirque. Jeremy went ahead to shoo the goats away from the trail so Zerc wouldn't freak out again, then we moved steadily up, climbing a thousand feet in about a mile toward Lincoln Pass. As the lake receded below us, we came even with its abrupt west end, where its outlet stream drops more than thirteen hundred feet over a series of cascades and Beaver Chief Falls, most of which we couldn't see for the intervening ridge and trees. It's not as hard a climb as Gunsight Pass, but for some reason Lincoln Pass is the one that reminded me of novelist and Glacier Park enthusiast Mary Roberts Rinehart's definition of a pass, written in 1918: "A pass is a thing which you try to forget at the time, and which you boast about when you get back home."

▲ *Mary Roberts Rinehart*

We moved north and west down from the pass, occasionally catching glimpses of Lake McDonald off to the west and stopping for some snacks and a chat with the keeper at Sperry Chalet, which was closed at the time for major refurbishing, so we missed having a taste of the small, comfortable society these great old chalets were famous for. We spent the early afternoon winding the five miles down Sprague Creek to Crystal Ford, then, conscious of the risk of a close encounter with a bear or two, we hiked very noisily through the thick, high, and very limited visibility scrub up Snyder Creek toward our third cirque at Snyder Lake.

On the trail, when we weren't taking pictures of the scenery, the llamas, or Kessie (all equally irresistible subjects), we were usually wondering about bears, especially on trails like this one, which was famous both for berries and bears. We were just a little late for the peak of berry season, but friends had told us the "hucks" should still be good. By now, Kessie had developed a keen eye for berries. From her perch in her little backpack she regularly directed whichever parent carried her to stop at this or that bush—a huck here, a thimbleberry there. Her face was often smeared purple, and all that sugar and goo sluiced through her agile young system at an alarming rate. The most pressing supply-related question of the trip was whether or not the diaper stock would hold out.

Sperry Chalet

▲ *Kestrel the Berry Girl*

But berries meant bears, especially here along Snyder Creek. I had every expectation of seeing some, or at least seeing what had sluiced through *their* systems.

Even aside from reading about the 1967 deaths of two hikers killed by bears in Glacier, it may be that the first specific natural history information I ever learned about Glacier had to do with its plants and its bears. In my first years as a ranger-naturalist in Yellowstone in the early 1970s, I often heard (and even repeated) the erroneous but popular common knowledge that Yellowstone was poor bear habitat when compared to a place like Glacier, because Glacier has *lots of berries.* The only thing that turned out to be true about that unfortunate local wisdom was the part about the berries. With its great herds of elk and bison, its native trout populations, and its grand smorgasbord of other bear foods, Yellowstone wasn't so much a less good bear habitat as it was just a very different bear habitat.

But it was true about Glacier's berries. When I was a child in Pennsylvania, my dad took us huckleberry picking in some great berry country, but I have to admit that when I walk the trails of Glacier, I've never seen anything like this. It isn't just that there are so many kinds—huckleberries, elderberries, raspberries, thimbleberries, kinnikinnik, serviceberries, strawberries, bunchberries, buffaloberries (to name only some of the ones you can eat and to ignore the ones you shouldn't)—but that there are so many of them out there. It is, without doubt, a great place to be a bear.

Grizzly country invites you to participate in a rich and thriving folklore, a near-mythology of nature that humans have constructed around the bear. Every bit of bear sign provides you with a link into that world, whether it scares the devil out of you, stirs your soul, or just gives you a laugh. One day at the Goat Haunt trailhead in Waterton I overheard some hikers excitedly reporting to a ranger about pile of bear scat they'd found on the trail a few miles away. The ranger calmly answered their questions and agreed with their wide-eyed assertions that sometimes the piles are "*REALLY BIG!*" but finally had to explain that you can't tell everything about a bear just by seeing a pile of poop. They were a little let down by the failure of this pile to provide a complete biography of the bear that produced it, but after a moment's thought, one of them said, "It does, however, answer the age-old question."

▲ *Hucks*

◀ *Thimbleberries*

Even though I can always get some storytelling mileage out of a grizzly bear encounter, I'm just as glad I didn't see any of them on this trip (every time Kessie called to one of us in that sweet, high-pitched little doll voice, I could imagine a bear or lion perking up its ears). What I saw instead was just as good. No, it was better.

Snyder Lake rests in a rounded bowl of rock, the lower of two small ponds nestled tightly in a dense forest on the cirque floor. It was a much more cramped feeling there than in the previous cirques, with the walls of rock looming straight up from the forest around us. When we arrived in the evening, I found it pretty gloomy. But in the morning, it seemed a place of great possibilities, and I eagerly glassed the little pockets of meadow high on the slopes for signs of wildlife. Then Marsha and I waited quietly in the morning chill at the little food preparation area not far from the campsites. We knew Kessie would roust her parents soon, and it was nice just to be awake, hungry, and waiting.

Idling there in mental neutral, I happened to be looking in the right direction when a tiny, dark weasel scooted out of the brush, climbed onto a log, and checked us out. Telling Marsha to look, I pulled my little camera from my pocket and ran off three or four hasty shots (they came out only good enough to prove I saw a weasel, showing its dark brown back and buff belly) before it ran back into the bushes. I see bears a lot more often than I see weasels, so my day was made almost before it began.

After a long, slow breakfast, at which we exchanged the sort of hygiene-related war stories that seem to come up toward the end of a long, bathless hike (Jeremy won with a tale of a month without a shower in the Himalayas), I took my little video camera for a walk to the far side of the pond, where a steep rock wall was crumbling into talus slopes right down to the water's edge. I wanted to get a look at the inlet stream, which emerged from a tight stone defile in the trees, but I never got that far.

▼ *Pika*

As I stopped to check the talus for pikas, whose little chirps of alarm I could hear, a larger, lighter weasel suddenly popped into view. I got about half a minute of wobbly video of this one as it launched itself across the talus, bounding from rock to rock, stopping here and there to poke its head up, and finally disappearing. A mountain lion sighting might have been more satisfying right then, but not much. I couldn't wait to get back to the others and brag.

THE INLAND COAST

Last mornings on hikes are complicated. I can't entirely prevent my mind
from looking ahead to what I'll be doing when I'm out of the backcountry, but I regret that the trip is over. (Jeremy observed, "By the time we
finish this hike, we'll be in good enough shape to start it.") By now we
were old hands at packing the llamas, who hummed softly as we did so.
When they hummed, we never knew for sure if they were objecting,
commiserating with one another, or even expressing enthusiasm that we
were on our way again. It almost seemed they knew, perhaps by the relative lightness of the load, that we were almost home. Kessie fueled up at
one final huckleberry bush, and we were on our way. It's only about four
miles from Snyder Lake to the trailhead at Lake McDonald, and it's all
downhill, so we were in for an easy hike.

    The last couple of miles were the most welcoming anyway, pass-
ing through the great cedar-hemlock forests that encircle the east end
of Lake McDonald. We were suddenly strolling through what appeared

▲ *Weasel*

Coastal Forest

to be a maritime forest, such as we would expect to see along the Pacific Coast, five hundred miles to the west. With its high precipitation, humid local climate, and moderate temperatures and wind speeds, this is one of the most surprising and refreshing walking areas in the park, whether on the trail down from Snyder Lake or on the nearby trail of the Cedars and the hike to Avalanche Lake.

At first, when I'm in a forest like this, I go through a stage of gaping at the grandness—the towering western hemlocks, whose trunks I always remember better than their soft, rubbery branches; the ragged-bark red cedars with their feathery branches so like the junipers close to my home in southwestern Montana; or the western larch, which interest me for their ponderosa-pine-like bark, their splaying branch arrangement, and their habit of shedding their needles every fall.

But after a few minutes, it starts to soak in that the big trees aren't really what set the mood here. It's the heavy, often-lush understory of the forest from which the big trunks emerge—not just the fern and maple and huckleberry and all the other shrubs but the ground-hugging plants as well. In fact, it may be these smallest plants that most inspire the cathedral image so often invoked to express the mood of these forests. Certainly the light filtering through the high boughs and architecturally uniform trunks of the trees bring to mind vaulted sanctuary ceilings and windows, but it's the 50 to 90 percent ground coverage of the mosses and the visual softening of the various hanging lichens and fungi that give these woods their reverential hush. And it's the startlingly fresh and distinctive song of the varied thrush, which I never hear without thinking of precisely this little stretch of forest, that somehow accentuates and completes that hush.

Varied Thrush

But now we're anxious to be out—to start sorting our gear from the panniers and otherwise preparing for the long drives home that we know face us later today. We lead the llamas down to the road, wait for a break in the traffic (jarring, noisy cars and road noise shock us after so many miles of soft llama tread), and cross to the lodge parking lot so we can unload. Larry Eddy, who dropped us and his wonderful llamas off five

▲ *Lake McDonald*

days earlier on the other side of the Continental Divide, shows up with his trailer right on time, listens calmly to our various adventures and revelations about goats, and accepts our thanks and a check. Then the llamas are quickly loaded and out of our lives before we even realize how much we'll miss them.

Almost immediately, for me at least, the country we've just crossed, with its lingering glaciers, bragging-size passes, bright-eyed wildlife, and smoke-tinted light, becomes a little unreal. When I have to describe Waterton-Glacier to someone who hasn't been there, my mind fills with the feelings of the country, and my mouth trips over inadequate adjectives. The magic of it never leaves me, but when I'm not there I'm haunted by the insufficiency of my memory to do it justice.

CHAPTER FIVE

Glacier Ghosts

CHIEF MOUNTAIN

I prefer to approach Glacier from the east. Driving across the high plains toward the Front Range, I find myself anxious to clear the final ridge that stands between me and my first glimpse of Chief Mountain. Glacier National Park shares this singular eminence with the Blackfeet Indian Reservation. Chief Mountain is a freestanding outlier of the great Lewis Overthrust, rising alone and imposing against the skyline near the Canadian border.

More important, it is a place of spiritual power. Nearly all the tribes and groups of Native Americans who had any contact with the region considered it so,

▲ *Backcountry Morning*

whether as a home to great spirits, a shrine, or a vision-questing site, and for more than two hundred years white travelers have noted it in their journals and books as a great and emotionally stirring landmark.

I agree, however, with the people—and I include here both Native Americans and those of us whose ancestors arrived more recently—who are quick to point out that visually extraordinary places like Chief Mountain, though indeed special or sacred, should never be seen as isolated islands of meaning and power in an otherwise unvalued landscape. Properly seen, Chief Mountain is more like a high point, literally and figuratively, in an entire landscape of natural and cultural richness.

Chief Mountain seems to dominate the landscape and attract the eye from whatever direction it is visible, and it is visible for a very long distance. To the east, when I'm out on the Blackfeet Reservation—up to the bottom of my heart in a trout lake—I seem always aware of it. Though I may be straining excitedly to cast far enough to reach the heavy rainbows that are slashing at emerging caddis flies, my sight is still drawn to the northwest and the mountain. To the west in the park, skirting Cosley Lake on the trail to the Belly River Ranger Station, I anticipate and then enjoy its emergence from behind Cosley Ridge. To the north, I am always amazed at how far into Canada I can travel and still see it, just a faint dot above the prairie horizon. And on any road along or out from the east side of the park, I often orient myself by it, casually but irresistibly checking to see if it's where I expect it to be on the horizon. Often it isn't quite where I thought, and I realign my mental compass, puzzling over how I got turned around.

It took me a while to realize that I wasn't attracted to this mountain just as a tourist, or out of respect for other peoples' spiritual attachment to it, or because of my interest in its more recent historical significance. It didn't matter what I knew or what spiritual tradition I was part of. This mountain commanded my attention and haunted my thoughts just because it is the kind of place that does that.

Chief Mountain reminds us of a fundamental fact of the Waterton-Glacier area: it may be authentic and uncompromising wilderness, but it is also a cultural landscape, preserving in its remote valleys ten thousand years of human history. People have been making the most of the present Waterton-Glacier area—hunting, fishing, gathering, enjoying all the sights, finding comfortable ground, crossing all the passes—more or less since the receding ice first permitted them

Weeping Wall

to. We have at times tended to forget the duration and thoroughness of the occupation of this landscape, but from the time of the earliest literature on the Waterton-Glacier region, at least a few commentators, including George Bird Grinnell, appreciated it. More than a century ago, Grinnell, quoting a sarcasm among unnamed old-timers, affirmed the ancient human heritage of this landscape:

> Mountain men have an old saying: "The deer made the first trails; the elk followed the deer, the buffalo the elk, and the Indians the buffalo; after the Indians came the trapper; then an army officer came along and discovered a pass."

After so many years of human occupation and so much spirituality, opinion, and folklore growing up around the features of this country, there is no clean separation between culture and nature. We are drawn to places like this as much for the shared human experience of them as for the wonder of their beauty or the challenging fascination of their ecological processes.

For better or worse, my culture has given me a great interest in discovery. I like to know who found a place, what they thought of it, and how they named it, especially a place as wonderful as this. But the written record tends to limit me to what the Euro-Americans did and thought. The people who were here for several hundred generations before that didn't leave me their story in nice tidy written form like the record left by the parade of early white travelers, so it's a little too easy to slight them in favor of the Fidlers, DeSmets, Pallisers, Grinnells, Pumpellys, and all the others I can connect with just by opening a book. Still, one of the most important and provocative books ever published about the Waterton-Glacier area, Brian Reeves and Sandra Peacock's *"Our Mountains Are Our Pillows": An Ethnographic Overview of Glacier National Park* (2001), does give today's bookish explorer an extraordinary glimpse into the world of those earlier generations.

I try to balance my passion for history with a like passion for personal impression. I will never experience this country quite the way an ancient Indian (or a modern one, for that matter) did. I will never see these parks through the eyes of a Victorian geologist. I don't need to. It helps me to know how they saw and used the place, but it's up to me to get what I can from it.

TO THE SUN

For all the grandeur and photogeneity of the hotels of Waterton-Glacier, they are not the most impressive human landmark here. That honor almost certainly belongs to a site that was placed on the National Register in 1983 and has the odd dimensions of thirty feet by almost fifty miles. Created in a time when extraordinary engineering projects seemed an appropriate feature of national parks, the Going-to-the-Sun Road was dedicated in July 1933 and has thrilled (even frightened) millions of visitors since.

Like it or not, this road turned Glacier from a wilderness park with border developments into a place that the average tourist could cross. Until this road over Logan Pass was open, the only way to experience the high passes or the steep slopes of the mountains was on foot or horseback. In 1933, all at once, anyone with a car or a bus ticket could do the trip in a couple of hours, with stops along the way for assorted wonders and an unrelieved series of stunning panoramas.

Perhaps if we had it to do over again today, we might not do it at all. At least there would be a whole lot more public conversation about the advisability and wisdom of cutting such a magnificent primitive setting in half, and about the ecological and social consequences of doing so. But this road is now a treasured cultural resource, one of those peculiar elements of some wilderness parks—a human achievement so distinguished and special that it becomes a significant part of the park experience.

MENUS

The road to Waterton Townsite and into the park crosses the Waterton River just below Lower Waterton Lake and along the edge of Maskinonge Lake. Not far from here, where the river emerges from the steep country and sets out across the prairie, there was once a large wintering campsite for native people whose sense of the seasons was far more sophisticated than mine. Back when it was open to fishing, I was unable to catch even one pike from Maskinonge Lake, but these folks often spent part of their year here, fishing and hunting successfully enough to prosper. We know from archeological work here that their prey included ungulates (deer, sheep, elk, moose, bison) who came here to winter, as well as a variety of furbearers (beaver, fox, wolf, coyote), quite a few species of birds (swans, ducks, and geese), and of course fish. As spring and summer came, the people followed the animals into higher country.

Archeologists have established that these seasonal movements were quite complicated, and not even consistent from year to year. The people of this region seemed to move around in ways that were resourceful rather than habitual. The Waterton-Glacier area was part of a complex set of opportunities that were exploited as need be, perhaps every year, perhaps every few years (you haven't really given yourself a chance to appreciate the richness of this region's native human cultures until you've visited the interpretive center and archeological site at Head-Smashed-In Buffalo Jump, a World Heritage Site near Fort Macleod, a little more than an hour north of Waterton). When these people found conditions not to their liking, they drew upon a vast store of regional knowledge and adapted.

Today, when I sit in the charming dining room of the Prince of Wales Hotel overlooking Waterton Townsite, I do my foraging less directly,

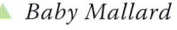

▲ *Baby Mallard*

through the dinner menu and the wine list. Gaping at the spectacular view of Upper Waterton Lake, I am supremely comfortable even though my own migration patterns are somewhat more erratic and less rational than those of earlier people.

But that is not to slight my culture's own traditions. White people have only been here a couple of hundred years, but this land has shaped our ways, too. I prefer the wilderness parts of the greater western parks, but I regularly require myself (this has gotten a lot easier as I have gotten older) to participate in the most intensely social traditions of these places, such as sit-down dinners with table cloths in nice hotels.

▲ *Prince of Wales Hotel*

For one thing, I must remind myself about where these parks came from. Waterton-Glacier, Yellowstone, and most of the other western parks originated in a fairly highbrow touristic tradition that was and

◀ *Lake McDonald Lodge*

is considerably older and more politically influential than their current backpacking tradition.

For another, it's fun to engage all the good things about these traditions of hospitality. A remarkably high percentage of the people who care for you in park hotels, dining rooms, and other facilities are genuinely excited to be there and eager to make sure you have a good time. There aren't all that many other businesses I will encounter in my life where I can go and be so sure of such an enthusiastic reception.

So while these grand old hotels may seem jarringly inappropriate to modern wilderness enthusiasts, they were central to the primary park experience for many generations. Many visitors to Waterton-Glacier in the early days found lodging in the boundary developments, from which they were launched in long, luxurious pack trains into the high country. The accounts written by these people suggest that one of the things they most enjoyed about the experience was the contrast: into the wild forest for the day but back to the refreshing antidote of resort life for a good dinner and a decent sleep each night.

▼ *Granite Park Chalet*

FAMILIAR TRAILS

And so I conduct my exploration in two ways. The first adventure is my own, out there along the rivers, roads, and trails. I have no illusion that it's a momentous or even distinguished adventure—I'm painfully aware of my limitations when it comes to the more arduous aspects of wilderness travel, for example—but for each of us the adventure is as big or as little as we make it, and imagine it.

The second adventure is vicarious, appreciating this place through the eyes and words of those who knew it earlier and better than I ever will. Wherever I have traveled in North America, I have found my own experiences fuller for knowing what previous travelers that way found, and thought, and felt. If I'm lucky enough, I will come upon the trail of Thoreau, or Lewis, or Leopold, or any of a thousand other great nature explorers who paved my way and now illuminate the scene for me. And if I don't find one of the great literary heroes of nature literature, I am sure to find plenty of specialized expertise; if you read carefully, the most arid, analytical scholarship has a poetry of its own.

For example, archeologists' reports, though often technical and scientifically conservative (lacking the satisfying conjecture and literary warmth that researchers abhor), are all I need to picture some of the realities of these long-passed families and their ways. Historians' overviews are also helpful sometimes, but I'm far more attracted to firsthand accounts. Reading along in some early travel account or explorer's journal, I make their discoveries again, along with some new ones.

Recently, while engaged in this kind of browsing at the wonderful special collections library at Montana State University, in Bozeman, I happened upon a small self-published book by Henry Klussman, *A Trip to the Northwest by Automobile* (1922). On page 45, I noticed a nice photograph of Gunsight Lake, taken from halfway up the trail to Gunsight Pass. But Klussman's Gunsight Lake of 1922 was different from the one I described in chapter 1. The shoreline I fished was lined with vegetation, but in the photograph it was lined with the buildings of a chalet, one of seven rustic backcountry Shangri-las that served riding and hiking tourists at the time. It's fashionable to consider the parks overdeveloped these days, and they are indeed struggling with ever larger crowds and commercial pressures, but in some ways they're probably less developed than they were half a century ago. Only two of those seven chalets, Sperry and Granite Park, remain, and one of the reasons I treasure their survival is

Beargrass

that they connect me to something that was once important, even precious, in my own culture.

Everywhere I turn in Waterton-Glacier, I encounter my predecessors. Kintla Lake, where I went to see the bull trout, was the site of the one of the first oil wells in Montana more than a century ago. Almost as long ago, near Many Glacier, where I have watched goats and grizzlies in almost complete solitude, a thousand people lived in the mining town of Altyn. Driving any of the roads, I meet a parade of named peaks, lakes, streams, and living things, each humanizing the landscape just a little.

And of course in every drainage, no matter how remote, the archeologist's eye might discern traces of the original human inhabitants of this country, some of whose ancestors still live nearby and hold to their own sense of the land's worth and power. When you travel here, you can enjoy being alone, or you can shift mental gears just a little and share the good company of ten thousand years of common experience.

MANNERS

And visiting a national park is all about company—wanted or unwanted, predictable yet surprising, full of hope, wonder, and a quirkiness that is probably behind most of humanity's unprecedented and hasty success as a species. It is a truism among park professionals that some significant percentage of visitors "don't know how to act." This is a cautionary phrase my mother often used to describe her children when we were acting badly; she meant, in fact, that we *did* know how to act but were acting otherwise and were doing so, it was to be understood, at some risk.

But when the phrase is used by rangers, it often means that the people in question literally are unaware of the proper way to behave. This distinction does not, however, relieve them of all responsibility for themselves, and it is still to be understood that they are at risk, either from the immediate consequences of their foolish behavior or from the ranger's discipline.

Tourist stories are the source of vast amusement among park staff, who, at their best, share them with a fine combination of exasperation and tolerance, knowing full well that we're all tourists somewhere and that national parks, though the most natural of places in some ways, are entirely and unfortunately *un*natural in most people's daily lives.

Patience is the key here, and patience most often means a tolerance for sharing. We were driving back from Cameron Lake to Waterton Townsite late one evening. Dusk was over and it was all but dark. There was only enough light to see that ahead a few cars were stopped on the road. As we approached and slowed, we could see a pair of young black bears in the grassy corridor bordering the road. As they moved along the corridor, cars stacked up behind the lead car, which moved along the corridor at the same speed as the bears, keeping them directly outside their windows. The occasional camera flash indicated that the people in that first car were excited about this nice opportunity to see black bears close up.

▲ *Black Bear Cub*

But they didn't share. Rather than take a reasonable turn and pull away, they succumbed to their good fortune and stuck right by the bears for several minutes, until the animals retreated into the forest. The people in the several following cars never got a good look, and the people in the first car probably didn't even realize that they had just hogged a special moment that they would better have shared.

Manners in a park require thought. They require attention to kindness when kindness is not even on your mind. One especially telling example: The moment's excitement at seeing something wonderful along a park road may make you hurry from your car, thoughtlessly slamming all the car's doors when such noise could at worst scare the wonderful thing away and at least spoil a quiet mood among the other people there. As you approach such a situation, think "shrine of beauty" rather than "tailgate party," and you'll never go wrong.

On the other hand, if you see others behaving poorly, patience and tolerance become even more important. It's hard not to take stupid, harmful behavior personally. But try to keep a little distance between your emotions and your observations. Introducing your self-righteous indignation into someone else's foolishness is known as "playing ranger." It can get you into all kinds of sudden and even awful trouble. The more serious the misbehavior, the harder you should think about exactly what your role might be. It's always a judgment call, of course, and some problems just can't wait. But as much as they might annoy us, most viola-tions of decent park manners probably aren't going to do as much harm to the park's real values as they are to our moment's experience. The person feeding the chipmunk, or deer, or bear; the thoughtless camper whose stereo is ruining the evening for her neighbors; the fast driver, the tree-chopper, the dog-releaser, the road hog, and all the others who interrupt the flow of satisfaction for those around them need help, guidance, and, in some cases, discipline. There are people trained to provide it.

STAKES

Parks test much more than our patience with each other. They test our ideas and our dreams. All our high-flown ambitions for the national parks come down to an endless series of immediate, complex, and probably irre-solvable issues that must be sorted out one at a time. Fire, bears, wolves, eagles, bull trout, mountain goats, and all the other pieces of the place demand the best thinking we can muster, and together they compel us to stretch our ideals and our perceptions in directions that were unimagi-nable to the parks' founders. Park management is necessarily on-the-job training, and visiting parks is always an opportunity for rumination as much as it is a chance for delight.

The American and Canadian national park movements, though they've proceeded by different paths, have shared important similari-ties. As experience accumulated, we've all had to revise not only our expectations but our hopes as well. We've had to replace the early idea of the parks—as places where nature could be manipulated and even "improved" as we chose—to something much harder to define: places where nature's freedom to make its own decisions about how the land-scape will look and change is a key element in why the park is worth hav-ing and enjoying.

We've also been compelled by the parks, and by similar wild-land reserves, to rethink our notion of where nature fits in the modern world, and vice versa. Entire academic disciplines have grown up in environmental ethics, ecological history, conservation biology, wild-life economics, and other essential fields that help us resolve just how parks fit in modern human culture and how modern human culture is a product and aspect of the wild nature that the parks try so hard and controversially to preserve. We are a long way from having answers, and among the disputants in the debates over these very big questions the disagreements seem only to become more pronounced.

But let's set all that aside for a moment and remember that parks can still test us on the most elemental level. Of course, even the hardiest and most adventurous backcountry adventurer rarely is up against genuine survival situations. Grizzly bear attacks, climbing accidents, and killer blizzards are all a lot more rare than auto accidents. Usually in the wilderness there are just gradations of personal responsibility at stake, and the only thing at risk is whatever illusions we have about our competence at getting along in the woods. It's certainly possible to do something fatally wrong in places like Waterton-Glacier, but that doesn't necessarily distinguish these places from the rest of the planet, except that in these parks if we get ourselves in a terrible fix it may take the helicopter a little longer to reach us.

So whether we care for parks abstractly, as great classrooms of ecological theory and cultural anthropology, or more personally, as places of personal or spiritual power, with each passing generation we have more need for them.

I have elsewhere written that the search for answers about our relationship with nature is probably more important than the answers themselves. No matter how confident any generation is that it now has things figured out, the next generation will show them up and demand new answers, or even ask new questions. If we exercise our finest ideals and deepest wisdom, we can get it right, but the next generation is going to have to get it right all over again for themselves.

TOYS AND TOOLS

The only part of backpacking that I really love is going down the trail. I just like being out there, whether trying to put on the miles or just moseying along. Glacier helped me recognize this on the llama trip I described in chapter 4. There is an inordinate satisfaction to be had in the hiker's precious self-sufficiency—of knowing that you are carrying everything you need, if only for the next couple of days—but when the llamas liberated me so completely from any excuse to haul that stuff on my back, I had to admit that the actual backpack had lost all its novelty for me. This business of being out there was no longer about backpacking; it was about the trail.

Even more, it was not about camping, which for me has always been what I must put up with until there's enough light so I can get back on the trail, or the trout stream, or whatever it is I really am there for.

At the same time, in a kind of abstract way, I must admit that I still enjoy the *idea* of backpacking, mostly because the backpack is full of so much neat stuff. Though never a true gear junkie, I do get a big kick out of all those little gadgets and doodads that generations of serious outdoorsmen have dreamed up to serve their wilderness needs. The entire Swiss Army can't have many more of their knives than I do, or more admire the self-reliance and competence so magnificently symbolized by one of those big, fat, dozen-bladed-scissored-screwdrivered-corkscrewed things as it rests heavily in my hand.

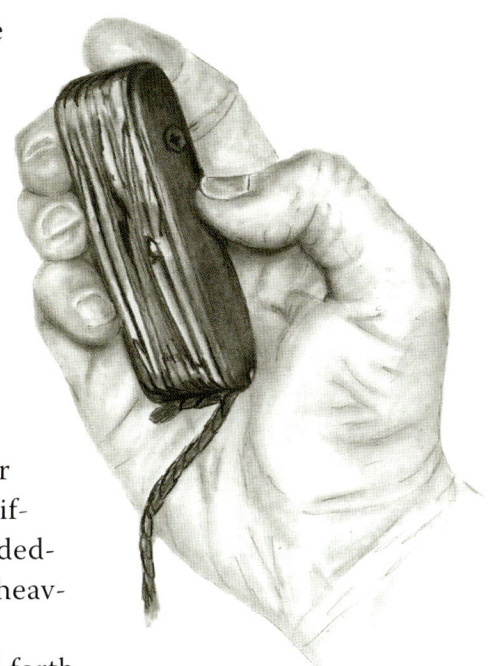

▲ *Handful of Reassurance*

I'm in the best company in this waffling back and forth on the matter of technology on the trail. In the middle of the last century, in *A Sand County Almanac* (1950), the great wildlife scientist and wilderness advocate Aldo Leopold struggled with striking the right balance between technology and simplicity in our nature recreations. He feared "the gadgeteers," who produced those little "contraptions, all offered as aids to self-reliance, hardihood, woodcraft, or marksmanship, but too often functioning as substitutes for them." I know about this fear. In almost forty years of fly fishing, my fishing vest has bloated and slimmed cyclically, as I first declared my independence from excess and then succumbed, nifty gadget by nifty gadget, to it again. I have gone through similar cycles of resistance and surrender with camera gear and wildlife-watching optics. There is no easy solution to these challenges. Even Leopold, among the wisest of all modern wilderness wanderers, admitted that when it came to the place of technology on the trail, he "did not pretend to know what is moderation."

Mark Johnson, a wildlife veterinarian and friend, and I arrived at Elizabeth Lake one afternoon, more tired than we would have wanted to admit after the hike in from Swiftcurrent. During our climb up to Ptarmigan Tunnel and then on down to the lake, I had achieved the pleasant stupor and near-incoherence one would rather have at the end of a trip than on the first night:

Paul: "What's for dinner?"
Mark: "Spaghetti."
Paul: "Great!" Short pause. "What's for dinner?"

For this trip I had invested in a brand-new, top-of-the-line backpacking stove, recommended in glossy magazines as the best, most reliable on the market. It was one of those dandy little units that vaguely resemble a NASA Lunar Excursion Module, except that it has more moving parts.

We dutifully tested it in Mark's backyard before the trip, and it worked fine (its dramatic capacity for making a column of flame also compared favorably with the LEM). Now, ten miles from the trailhead and thus safe from replacement, it wouldn't work at all. Squatting there at the group food-preparation area, in full embarrassing view of other campers who were intermittently firing up their own stoves, we fussed unprofitably with the thing for an hour or so, until Mark, who has to deal with numerous high-strung little medical instruments, patiently disassembled the whole apparatus and nursed it back to a kind of fire-sputtering health.

Meanwhile, we struck up a conversation with a young, but well-outfitted, couple who had watched this whole performance. They laughed philosophically and said that they had the very same kind of stove and that it was so unreliable that they actually carried two, just so they'd have parts and backup.

What impressed me about this statement was the cheerful fatalism of their remarks. They regarded their problematic little LEM, in firm agreement with the magazines, as a "good stove." Only having to carry two of them to do the job of one was apparently something they saw as a real advantage—a major selling point in the stove's favor. It was all so far from the commercial images of the happy hikers instantly starting up their trustworthy little stoves that it reminded me of similar commercial fantasies I see constantly in my favorite fly-fishing magazines, in which people make perfect long casts with all their expensive gear. The line turns over with smooth precision, the fly floats upright, the waders never leak, and the fish rise like they're hired.

Just for this trip, I had also invested in a similarly top-rated water filter that self-destructed the next day. The engineering of this little machine was so perverse as to border on the insane. It consisted mainly of a small plastic chamber through which stream or lake water was forced and filtered by means of a hand-operated push-pull pump unit. The rod that drove the pump, the single most stressed part of the mechanism, had, for apparently cosmetic reasons, been made of two differently colored sections of plastic tubing that promptly fell apart. We spent the rest of the trip patching the thing together, shimming it here and there with little fragments of our backcountry permit to try to keep some pressure in it, and frequently dismantling it so we could reassemble the weak pieces. It met every sensible definition of junk.

I always learn things in national parks, and I learned a lot from these experiences. Mark, who displayed a deliberative, almost Taoist, calm each time he sat down and spread out the pieces of the stove or the water filter, taught me about going with the problem rather than fighting against it. More helpfully, he taught me to look for high spring sites, whose water had just emerged from some rocky slope and had low odds of carrying any of those nasty organisms that we needed the pathetic filter to protect us from.

I also was reminded that there is much to be said for overpowering a problem with the simplest answer. We camped a couple of nights with a party of three or four robust fellows who dined on massive quantities of Spam and real eggs (they carried the eggs, all sloshing around together, in a huge plastic water bottle). They had a "stove" that looked like an obese propane torch. Bereft of anything even vaguely sophisticated or high-tech, this device featured one simple on-off valve. It roared instantly into blazing action, and its big bright jet of flame would cook things at a considerable distance. I like to think that Leopold, and all the other ghosts who inhabit the historic trails in our parks, would have approved.

HEARTS AND EAGLES

As much as I used to like to think of myself as a wilderness kind of guy, I must confess that I'm a typically socialized, commerce-adapted product of my heavily populated world. The older I get, the more I love to wander through the great old park hotels, and I never miss a chance to cruise

The International,
Waterton Lake ▶

▲ *Red Bus*

the visitor centers and museums. Marsha's influence as an expert shopper has even turned me into a passable consumer at the gift shops.

I'm not really here to deny my technological addictions; I am always happily distracted when one of those lovely red buses goes by, and I've never been on a boat of any kind anywhere that I admired more than venerable *International* that has several times taken me to Goat Haunt at the south end of Waterton Lake. These experiences are all wonderful comforts, as is my ongoing quest for the perfect store-bought huckleberry milkshake.

But when I'm out in some isolated place in the parks with a spotting scope or a fly rod or a backpack, I still flinch a little when I hear voices approaching. It has often occurred to me that my aversion to society in these parks is nearly bizarre, considering that as a writer I not only need all those people as an audience, but I am celebrating (and therefore promoting) the very places I enjoy most when I have them to myself.

I certainly didn't have the parking lot at Logan Pass to myself on a darkly overcast late fall day, with lowering clouds driven hard by a snow-cold west wind. As late in the season as it was, there were still dozens of cars in the parking lot, with people hurrying to and from the shelter of

Waterton Lake from Bertha Lake Trail

the Visitor Center. A van-load of young hikers pulled into the parking spot next to mine, and a tall, leggy young woman hopped out and immediately responded to the dramatic chill by deciding to add a layer. As her companions rooted busily through their stuff for cameras and jackets, she quickly removed her boots and jeans, danced unaffectedly and pinkly around in the icy wind while she extracted a pair of tights from a pack and put them on and then restored her jeans and boots.

As more people got in and out of their cars, I focused on the distance, scanning the fabulous peakscape of this most famous of Glacier

Park passes. To the west, I picked a fast-flying eastbound eagle out of the confusion of grayish sky and snow-patched peaks. The bird's velocity was unbelievable. Outrunning the wind, it crossed over the divide above us and seemed to fast-forward to the east, shrinking smaller and smaller until I lost it in the cross-hatched snow patterns of Heavy Runner Mountain.

It was a moment just between me and the eagle, yet shared with a few others who happened to look up right then, yet entirely missed by many others who didn't happen to be looking up right then (or who were still watching to see what the girl might do next). Those of us who saw the eagle's flight exchanged a few smiles, but we didn't say a word to each other, and what could we possibly say to the ones who missed it?

It was not a moment for a camera or quantifying field notes. It was not something that would advance science or yield to analysis. It was not a shared thrill that required social celebration or the rhetorical applause of happy conversation.

It was instead the connection we are, after all, out there seeking, when the door opens for an instant on some greater truth—the kind of wisdom that eludes us if we try convert into words a thing whose only real value is as untranslated experience.

Come to this high, wild country with your heart open for that, and everything else it has to offer will be yours as well.

Acknowledgments

AUTHOR'S ACKNOWLEDGMENTS

My foremost gratitude is to my spouse and hero, Marsha Karle, who shared many of the experiences recounted in this book and continues to share a love of the wild beauty of Waterton-Glacier.

This book originally appeared, with a considerably shorter text, in 1996, when it was published as *Glacier & Waterton: Land of Hanging Valleys* (Tehabi Books/HarperCollins San Francisco). I'm especially grateful to Nancy Cash, Tom Lewis, and all the folks at Tehabi for making this such a fine experience, and to Jeff Garton, whose outstanding photographs illustrated that edition. The following acknowledgments, however, integrate people who helped with either the original or the present edition.

The staffs of Montana State University Library, Bozeman, and the Yellowstone National Park Research Library, Yellowstone Park, Wyoming, were enormously helpful with tracking down older or obscure items of value. A special note of thanks to Kim Allen Scott, Special Collections Librarian at MSU., for his help with illustration work. Beth Dunagan at the Glacier Park Library repeatedly located this or that essential document or book for me, and guided my use of that park's splendid collection.

Over the past thirty years or so, many other people have improved my appreciation of Waterton-Glacier with shared insights, suggestions, company, information, snacks, favors, and trails: Larry Aiuppy, Wendy Baylor, Wayne Brewster, Steve Frye, Jeff Garton, Melissa Garton, Steve Gniadek, Bob Haraden, Brace Hayden, Steve Herrero, Mark Johnson, Kate Kendall, Sandra Key, Suzanne Lewis, Leo Marnell, Sean Meegan, Dave Mihalic, Gary Moses, Alex Philp, Jeremy Schmidt, Kestrel Schmidt, Susan Sindt, Amy Vanderbilt, and Linda Wiggins. The helpfulness of the staffs of the National Park Service and Parcs Canada, as well as the staffs of any number of local businesses, was all any stranger could hope for.

The kind hospitality of Gary Moses and Amy Vanderbilt and Dave Mihalic made otherwise complicated plans simple, and much more fun.

Larry Eddy of Painted Sky Llama Ranch introduced us to his patient, companionable, and endlessly entertaining animals, Miles, Zerc, Petey, and Pinball, whom I could never thank adequately; after all, they brought the wine.

I am an enthusiastic member of the Glacier Natural History Association, and you should be, too. Learn more about their important programs and services by contacting them at the Glacier Natural History Association, Historic Depot, Highway 2, P.O. Box 310, West Glacier, MT 59936, www.glacierassociation.org.

ARTIST'S ACKNOWLEDGMENTS

I can't believe we actually got to do this project! My everlasting appreciation to the love of my life and my very best friend, Paul Schullery, who has supplied encouragement and support of my art and is my greatest fan.

My thanks to Clark Whitehorn at the University of New Mexico Press for his appreciation and enthusiasm for my artwork—and not minding my dumb questions.

Thanks especially to Susan Blackwood for her constant enthusiasm and inspiration and for the encouragement she has given to all her art students over the years.

I'm so grateful to my art critique group friends Justine Heisel, Bette Jaedicke, Anita Saunders, Rose Toth, and Priscilla Westesen who during our monthly meetings help me look harder and more critically at my own work and were always enthusiastic about this project.

Photographs taken on our many travels in Waterton-Glacier served as my primary resource for the art in this book, but I'm grateful to the following offices and individuals who provided additional images and support materials. Bill Hayden and Ellen Blickham of the National Park Service patiently assisted my use of the Glacier National Park photo files. Also in Glacier, Amy Macleod and Kate Kendall of the U.S. Geological Survey provided many helpful photographs of the grizzly bear hair snare research project. Yellowstone's on-line public domain photo files, created and managed by Jim Peaco of the National Park Service, provided several key images. Others whose photography, or help in locating pictures, was important to us included Judy Jennings, Lynn Kaeding, Ray Paunovich, and John Varley.

For my pencil portrait of Mary Roberts Rinehart, our friend Rick Rinehart, of Roberts Rinehart Publishers, granted permission for use of the charming photograph of her "roughing it" that appeared in her book *Nomad's Land* (1926). The portrait of the female grizzly bear, "Miss November," is from the collection of our friend Jon Catton.

Thanks also to the friends who have continued to share, discuss, collect, and otherwise support my artwork over the past ten years: Roger Anderson, Cynthia Andrus, Rick Balkin, Carol and Bob Barbee, Laurie Blue, Eleanor Clark, Rhoda Coleman, Jane and Ron Lerner, Gary and Cheryl Matthews, Suzanne Lewis, Sandra Nykerk, Vickie Raisler, Carol Shively, Henry Shovic, Debb Rodgers, Judith Schnell, Amy Vanderbilt, Frank and Judy Walker, Kate Wiggins and many others including all my friends at the Bozeman Chapter of the Montana Institute of the Arts.

Most especially, thanks to my mother, Dorothy Karle Griffith, who has always just wanted me to be happy—and I am!

Appendix

If you are new to the literature of Waterton-Glacier, I envy you the discoveries ahead. This is the briefest outline of some favorite publications and other information sources related to Waterton-Glacier. Many of these titles include large bibliographies and reference lists that will lead you to much other wonderful reading.

THE WEB

First, for those who can make the World Wide Web function to their advantage, here are a few important web sites to consider. The official Web sites of Glacier National Park, http://www.nps.gov/glac/, and Waterton Lakes National Park, http://www.pc.gc.ca/pn-np/ab/waterton/index_e.asp, are the best places to start for reliable information about the parks, whether your interest is in research, management, or just visiting.

The two parks' natural history associations publish and sell many fine publications. These nonprofit associations are important friends of the parks, so check out their offerings at the Glacier Natural History Association, http://www.glacierassociation.org/store/, and the Waterton Natural History Association, http://www.wnha.ca/publications.html. Better yet, stop at their visitor centers and browse the selection, then join either or both association and support their good work.

There are many other excellent and helpful informational Web sites that concentrate either on the Waterton-Glacier area or on issues of special importance to the area. Here are just a few. At Glacier National Park, the Crown of the Continent Research Learning Center, http://www.nature.nps.gov/learningcenters/index.cfm, has for several years published wonderful newsletters and reports on recent research and management issues in the region. The Crown of the Continent Ecosystem Education Consortium, http://www.crownofthecontinent.org/coceec.htm, takes a big-picture view of the region, and the Yellowstone To Yukon Conservation Initiative, http://www.y2y.net, takes an even bigger-picture view of the Rocky Mountains from Wyoming to northern British Columbia.

CULTURE

Web sites are only the beginning in learning about Waterton-Glacier. Providing a brief "bookshelf" of titles (and maybe a few more Web sites) is perhaps most helpful because the books listed here will provide a wealth of other sources, especially technical articles and reports from many disciplines. Historical works on Waterton-Glacier abound. Authoritative studies of native people and their long residence in the region include Brian Reeves and Sandra Peacock, *"Our Mountains Are Our Pillows": An Ethnographic Overview of Glacier National Park* (West Glacier, MT: National Park Service, 2001); and Brian O. K. Reeves, *Mistakis: The Archeology of Waterton-Glacier International Peace Park, Archeological Inventory and Assessment Program, 1993–1996*, edited by Leslie B. Davis and Claire Bourges, vols. 1 and 2 (Glacier National Park: National Park Service, 2003). An advantage of these volumes is that through them a host of native voices past and present are given room to speak at length on the land and their place in it. Among the many popularly written works relating to native people in and around Waterton-Glacier, see James Willard Schultz, *Signpost of Adventure: Glacier National Park as the Indians Know It* (Boston: Houghton Mifflin, 1926), and *Blackfeet Tales of Glacier National Park* (Helena: Montana Historical Society and Riverbend Publishing, 2002 edition of 1916 original); Adolf Hungry Wolf, *Good Medicine in Glacier National Park* (Skookumchuck, BC: Good

Medicine Books, 1971); and Dave Shea, *Chief Mountain: Home of the Thunderbird* (Myrtle Point, OR: Myrtle Point Printing, 2007).

For the history of Waterton Lakes National Park, see Graham A. MacDonald, *Where the Mountains Meet the Prairie: A History of Waterton Country* (Calgary, AB: University of Calgary Press, 2000). For a fascinating and timely cross section of perspectives on the park and surrounding area, see also B. Grinder, Valerie Haig-Brown, and K. Van Tighem, eds., *Voices in the Wind: A Waterton-Glacier Anthology* (Waterton Lakes, AB: Waterton Natural History Association, 2000).

General histories of Glacier National Park include Donald H. Robinson, edited and with new material by Maynard C. Bowers, *Through the Years in Glacier National Park* (West Glacier, MT: Glacier Natural History Association, 1970 reprint of 1960 original); C. W. Buchholtz, *Man in Glacier* (West Glacier, MT: Glacier Natural History Association and National Park Service, 1976); and C. W. Guthrie, *Glacier National Park: The First 100 Years* (Helena, MT: Farcountry Press, 2008).

Two recent books have focused on the Going-to-the-Sun Road: Rose Houk, *Going-to-the-Sun: The Story of the Highway Across Glacier National Park* (Englewood, CO: Woodlands Press, in conjunction with the Glacier Natural History Association, 1984); and C. W. Guthrie, *Going to the Sun Road: Glacier National Park's Highway to the Sky* (Helena, MT: Farcountry Press, 2006). For a finer appreciation of the high point on that road, see Jerry DeSanto, *Logan Pass: Alpine Splendor in Glacier National Park* (Guilford, CT: Falcon Guides, 1995). The role of the Northern Pacific Railway in the development and enjoyment of Glacier is the subject of C. W. Guthrie, *All Aboard! for Glacier: The Great Northern Railway and Glacier National Park* (Helena, MT: Farcountry Press, 2004).

The origin and accomplishment of the peace park is chronicled in Chris Morrison, *Waterton-Glacier International Peace Park: Born of a Vision* (Waterton Park, AB: Waterton Natural History Association and Pincher Creek Rotary Club, 2007).

Enjoyable stories of hotels in and near Waterton-Glacier include Ray Djuff and Chris Morrison, *View with a Room: Glacier's Historic Hotels & Chalets* (Helena, MT: Farcountry Press, 2001); Ray Djuff, *High on a Windy Hill: The Story of the Prince of Wales Hotel* (Calgary, AB: Rocky Mountain Books, 1999); and Gail Shay Atkinson and Jim Atkinson, *Izaak Walton Inn: A History of the Izaak Walton Inn and Essex, Montana* (Essex, MT: The authors and Izaak Walton Inn, 1995).

The art history of Glacier National Park is beautifully conveyed by Larry Len Peterson, *The Call of the Mountains: The Artists of Glacier National Park* (Tucson, AZ: Settlers West Galleries, 2002).

Among the other books relating to the history of Waterton-Glacier are Warren L. Hanna, *Stars over Montana: Men Who Made Glacier National Park History* (Glacier National Park, MT: Glacier Natural History Association, 1988); Robert C. Gildart, *Montana's Early-Day Rangers* (Helena, MT: Montana Magazine, 1985); Gerald A. Diettert, *Grinnell's Glacier: George Bird Grinnell and Glacier National Park* (Missoula, MT: Mountain Press, 1992); and Jack Holterman, *Place Names of Glacier/Waterton National Parks* (Helena, MT: Falcon Press, 1985).

NATURE

The geological story of Waterton-Glacier International Peace Park is told in Ann G. Harris, Esther Tuttle, and Sherwood D. Tuttle, *Geology of National Parks* (Dubuque, IA: Kendall/Hunt, 1997); Omar B. Raup, R. L. Earhart, James W. Whipple, and P. E. Carrara, *Geology Along the Going-to-the-Sun Road, Glacier National Park* (West Glacier, MT: Glacier Natural History Association, 1983); David Alt and Donald W. Hyndman, *Roadside Geology of Montana* (Missoula, MT: Mountain Press, 1986); and Ben Gadd, *Handbook of the Canadian Rockies* (Jasper, AB: Corax Press, 2000).

For the pressing issue of climate change, see the Climate Change in Mountain Ecosystems Web site of the USGS, http://www.nrmsc.usgs.gov/research/global.htm. The larger context and meaning of climate change as a factor in receding glaciers is the subject of Ben Orlove, Ellen Wiegandt, and Brian H. Luckman, *Darkening Peaks: Glacier Retreat, Science, and Society* (Berkeley: University of California Press, 2008).

Of books about Waterton-Glacier's life communities (both wild and human), I must begin with a singularly significant one. I imagine it to be the most valuable book ever published on the meaning and future of this region: Tony Prato and Dan Fagre, *Sustaining Rocky Mountain Landscapes: Science, Policy, and Management for the Crown of the Continent Ecosystem* (Washington, DC: Resources for the Future, 2007). The papers in this milestone work, covering archeology, economics, recreation, biodiversity, climate change, fire, and other essential topics, make up an unparalleled one-volume profile of the natural and cultural issues of the area, and the references in those papers will lead interested readers to every corner of the intellectual arena of the Northern Rockies. Among the other ecosystem-scale studies is Joseph L. Sax and Robert B. Keiter, "Glacier National Park and Its Neighbors: A Study of Federal Interagency Relations," *Ecology Law Quarterly* 14 (1987): 207–63.

Excellent general natural histories of the area include George C. Ruhle's long-admired *The Ruhle Handbook: Roads and Trails of Waterton-Glacier National Parks* (Minneapolis, MN: John W. Forney, 1972); Greg Beaumont, *Many-Storied Mountains: The Life of Glacier National Park* (Washington, DC: Natural History Series Division of Publications, National Park Service, 1978); and David Rockwell, *Glacier: A Natural History Guide* (Guilford, CT: Falcon Guides, 2007). Though it does not claim to cover the U.S. Glacier National Park, Ben Gadd's wonderful *Handbook of the Canadian Rockies*, mentioned above, provides a one-volume overview of the important elements of geophysical and natural history of the Northern Rockies.

In the text, I invoke the admirable and pathbreaking early work of Vernon Bailey and Florence Merriam Bailey, *Wild Animals of Glacier National Park: The Mammals and the Birds* (Washington, DC: U.S. Government Printing Office, 1918). Though its information has been replaced and improved upon in many specifics, the book is still fascinating both for its value as a historic document and for its prevailing natural history thought of the time.

For plants, see Richard J. Shaw and Danny On, *Plants of Waterton-Glacier National Parks and the Northern Rockies* (Missoula, MT: Mountain Press, 1979); Shannon Fitzpatrick Kimball and Peter Lesica, *Wildflowers of Glacier National Park* (Helena, MT: Riverbend Publishing, 2005); and Peter Lesica, *A Flora of Glacier National Park, Montana* (Corvallis: Oregon State University Press, 2002). For authoritative information and many references relating to whitebark pine and its important and dramatically changing role in the high country, you might start with the Whitebark Pine Ecosystem Foundation, http://whitebarkfound.org/nut-notes.html, which publishes a splendid newsletter.

There are some surprising vacant niches in the current library of books relating to Waterton-Glacier. Enterprising and ambitious nature writers should look to these opportunities. Though there are a number of fine books about bears that include Waterton-Glacier in their scope, it is especially puzzling that no one has written a book solely about the bears of this region—at least since Warren L. Hanna, *The Grizzlies of Glacier*

(Missoula, MT: Mountain Press, 1978), which was primarily an informal history of some of the most famous bear-human encounters in the park's history. Considering the richness of the anthropological, historical, and scientific information now available on the grizzly and black bears of Waterton-Glacier, it is bewildering that no such book has appeared. The volume of excellent scientific information now available is suggested by the Web site of the Northern Divide Grizzly Bear Project of the USGS, http://nrmsc.usgs.gov/research/NCDEbeardna.htm. For current information on grizzly bear management in the lower forty-eight states, visit the Web site of the Interagency Grizzly Bear Committee management team with oversight for grizzly bear recovery, http://www.igbconline. org. In the meantime, those interested in hiking safely in grizzly bear country have several excellent options among books devoted to the subject. The all-time best-seller among them and the book most respected among bear biologists and bear management professionals for its masterful explanation of why bears behave the way they do around people is Steve Herrero's classic *Bear Attacks: Their Causes and Avoidance* (New York: Lyons Press, 1985).

In addition to the early book by Bailey and the natural history books already mentioned, there are numerous exhaustive national or western U.S. mammal-related field guides that serve the Waterton-Glacier visitor well. Among books that treat a specific species of mammal, Douglas Chadwick, *A Beast the Color of Winter—The Mountain Goat Observed* (San Francisco, CA: Sierra Club Books, 1983), has proven an enduring tribute to Waterton-Glacier's iconic mammal and also a recognized classic of regional natural history.

For birds, besides the now somewhat dated monograph by Lloyd P. Parratt, *Birds of Glacier National Park*, Special Bulletin no. 9 (West Glacier, MT: Glacier Natural History Association, 1973 reprint of 1964 original), see Terry McEneaney, *Birding Montana* (Guilford, CT: Globe Pequot Press, 1998), and any of the national or regional bird field guides.

For fishes, an important early monograph is Leonard P. Schultz, *Fishes of Glacier National Park Montana*, USDI Conservation Bulletin (Washington, DC: U.S. Government Printing Office, 1941). General reference books include George Holton and Howard Johnson, *Field Guide to Montana Fishes* (Helena, MT: Falcon Press, 2001); and Robert Behnke, *Trout and Salmon of North America* (New York: Simon & Schuster, 2002). Fishermen may also wish to refer to Paul Hintzen, *Fishing Glacier National Park* (West Glacier, MT: Glacier Natural History Association,

1992); and Russ Schneider, *Fishing Glacier National Park* (Helena, MT: Falcon Press, 2002).

For the nearly continental-scale perspective of the Yellowstone-to-Yukon conservation initiative, see Douglas Chadwick, *Yellowstone to Yukon: National Geographic Destinations Series* (Washington, DC: National Geographic Society, 2000); and Florian Schulz, *Yellowstone to Yukon: Freedom to Roam* (Seattle, WA: Braided River, 2008).

Index